D0971614

The Competitive Power of Constant Creativity

The Competitive Power of Constant Creativity

Clay Carr

American Management Association

New York • Atlanta • Boston • Chicago • Kansas City • San Francisco
Washington, D.C. • Brussels • Mexico City • Tokyo • Toronto

This publication is designed to provide accurate and authoritative information in regard to the subject matter covered. It is sold with the understanding that the publisher is not engaged in rendering legal, accounting, or other professional service. If legal advice or other expert assistance is required, the services of a competent professional person should be sought.

Library of Congress Cataloging-in-Publication Data

Carr, Clay, 1934–
     The competitive power of constant creativity/Clay Carr.
     p.   cm.
     Includes bibliographical references and index.
     ISBN 0-8144-0225-9
     1. Creative ability in business.   2. Competition.   I. Title.
HD53.C38   1994   93-43674
658—dc20   CIP

Printing number

10   9   8   7   6   5   4   3   2   1

Contents

Preface

Should You Read This Book?

My first obligation as an author is to help you decide whether this book is for you. If you are a manager in an organization that does anything more than repetitive, routine work, you will find something in here that will be helpful. If you are a supervisor in manufacturing, with mainly traditional blue-collar workers reporting to you, it may give you some useful ideas. However, the book will be most valuable to you if you fit any of these descriptions:

1. You are the owner and/or CEO of a small- to medium-size company that is beginning to feel bureaucratic hardening of the arteries set in.
2. You manage "knowledge workers" (such as systems analysts, lawyers, engineers, financial analysts, human resource management specialists) and want to increase their effectiveness.
3. You are a manager at any level in a company that has been trying to adopt new methods of organization, such as self-managing teams, a very flat organizational structure, or serious process reengineering. If these are succeeding, this book will help you benefit even more from them. If they are not, it will help you use some of these methods in a different and perhaps more promising way.
4. You manage a blue-collar operation that is implementing automated systems, so that your performers are rapidly becoming more technicians than workers. The old ways of

organizing work and supervising aren't working very well anymore, and you're looking for more-effective ways.

5. You manage a public or nonprofit organization and are under pressure—or have the opportunity—to try nontraditional ways of accomplishing your mission.

6. Or you are in any other situation where the pressure is on, competition is tough, and you need to find new ways of operating just to keep up.

Let me be clear, though: This is not a survival manual. This is a *success* manual. The reason is simple. Read almost any book you want on management in the 1990s and you will find these four commandments: Do it fast. Do it with high quality. Do it at lower cost. And customize it for individuals or small groups of customers. That's what everyone is trying to do to stay competitive.

The ideas in this book will give you something your competitors aren't using: constant creativity. Your organization can use this creativity to develop new practices and processes that will speed up your offerings, increase their quality, cut their costs, and customize your products or services more easily. You can use it on your products and services to load them with more features your customers want. Most of all, you can use it to come up with *new* products and services—and stay one step ahead of your competitors.

What Will You Learn?

This book won't tell you for the umpteenth time how competitive your world is. You know that already. It won't rehash why organizations are so often uncreative. (If you want to read about that, see the first part of Karl and Steven Albrecht's *The Creative Corporation*.) Perhaps most surprising of all, the book doesn't contain a single creativity exercise. You can find such exercises in a wide variety of books, such as Part 2 of the Albrechts' book, Arthur VanGundy's *Idea Power* (which also has a list of PC programs to support creativity), and Michael Michalko's *Thinkertoys* (a book of wall-to-wall hands-on exercises).

This book takes a very different approach. It doesn't begin by asking what individuals have to do to be creative. Instead, it asks: What does an *organization* have to do to be a creative organization? If the organization is creative, its members will do their jobs creatively. They will set themselves goals that require creativity to accomplish. They will find opportunities where other organizations see only problems to be avoided or conditions to be endured.

How do you transform your organization into a constantly creative one? The answers to this question fall into four groups:

1. Chapters 1 through 4 deal with the basics—the core qualities of a constantly creative organization; how an organization operates as a creative system; how to avoid being framelocked and framebound; and how to use diversity and conflict to support creativity.
2. Chapters 5 through 7 tackle three problems that confront a creative organization—how to combine technology with creativity; how a creative organization can operate efficiently and reliably; and the kind of human resources management system a creative organization needs to support it.
3. Chapters 8 and 9 deal with the relationship between creativity and two of today's most prominent management themes—how to use teams creatively, and why a learning organization must be a creative organization.
4. Then, in the final chapter, we confront the most basic topic of all: how to manage so that you develop and maintain a constantly creative organization. Among other things, you'll discover that creative organizations cannot be managed—they can only be *led*.

A Word About Words

Let me explain several words I use in the book. I have chosen to call my goal the constantly *creative* organization. I could just as easily have called it the constantly *innovative* organization or the constantly *inventive* organization. Any of the three would work, and if you prefer one of the other terms to *creative* please think it each time you read *creative*. I chose *creative* for a simple reason: Both innovation and invention are associated with the creation of *products*, and this book concerns far more than how to develop new products.

You may also be surprised that while I often talk of managing I seldom talk of *managers*—and almost never of employees or workers. In a creative organization, as in any empowered organization, *everyone* is truly a manager. Some few may manage or at least lead others, but everyone manages himself or herself. This isn't a trivial distinction; an organization that still thinks in terms of managers and employees creates a sizable block to its own creativity.

So what terms do I use? When I look at a creative organization, I see *players*, *performers*, and *members*. The term I most prefer is *player*, because a successful company needs everyone to be a committed player every bit as much as a successful football team does. In the same vein, it needs everyone to be a performer who contributes to the organization's mission. And all of us need to see ourselves as members of the organization, not merely as hired hands.

One last word. Writing nonsexist language is a challenge, because English was constructed with the masculine pronoun as a synonym for human being. On occasion in the past, I have tried to use "he or she," "himself or herself," and other similar combinations. I do not like them. Consequently, throughout this book I alternate masculine and feminine pronouns, using both to refer to either sex.

And Now to Close the Opening

Two quick final points. First, this is not primarily an "idea" book. I hope it contains good ideas, and that they excite you. But ideas without concrete application aren't much more than entertainment. So you'll find that almost every chapter has very specific suggestions about *how* to develop and maintain a constantly creative organization. Some of the suggestions involve major steps; others require actions you can accomplish in a week or two. But I've tried my best to make them as practical and helpful as I could, drawing both on my own experience and on that of others.

Second, as I hope you've already noticed, I try to write as though we were sitting in comfortable chairs, talking with one another. Pedestals are uncomfortable; besides, I fell off the only one I own years ago. I'm like you. Every day I struggle to keep operations running smoothly, fight a fire or two—and still have the chance to improve what I and my organization do. The best I can do is share with you some of my observations and point you in directions that may be helpful to you. If that sounds worthwhile, please join me as we explore what it means to be a constantly creative organization.

Acknowledgments

First, to Greywolf, founder of Aesculapia Wilderness Retreat, who reminded me that creativity is the wellspring of all life (and, not incidentally, enabled me to halt the progress of a serious illness in the process).

To Warner Books for permission to quote the incident of Dale and Ben in Chapter 1 from *Rivethead*, Ben Hamper's remarkable book about life on the automotive assembly line.

To Adrienne Hickey, as professional and helpful an editor as an author could want.

To Mike Snell, an equally professional and helpful literary agent. (This is the fifth book for which Mike must share at least some of the blame.)

To Boyd Richards, editor of *Performance Improvement Quarterly*, for publishing my article "Diversity and Performance: A Shotgun Marriage?" in the Fall 1993 issue. The material on diversity in Chapter 4 is excerpted from this article.

To Sivasailam Thiagarajan, former editor of *Performance & Instruction*, who has not only published a number of my articles but helped me learn how to pronounce his name in the process.

To Ricardo Semler, whose leadership at Semco (São Paulo, Brazil) made it one of the clearest examples of a constantly creative organization there is. Unfortunately, his book *Maverick* appeared too late for me to reference it.

And, always, to Gayle, my wife—to whom I have yet to say, "You just don't understand me!"

Chapter 1
What Makes an Organization Creative?

If you don't have a competitive advantage, don't compete.
—Jack Welch, CEO, General Electric

Welcome to the red-hot nineties! Competition rises to a fever pitch. Established companies suddenly plunge deeply into the red. They wrestle with downsizing and restructuring (to the point that one stressed-out manager exclaimed "We downsized or rightsized appropriately. What we're doing now is just trying not to capsize").[1] At the same time, they try to focus on and serve rapidly changing markets. Successful organizations explore dramatically new forms of organization; networked organizations suddenly appear, even virtual corporations. Blue-collar workers are replaced by technicians supported by an increasing investment in information technology. Land, labor, and capital are available to entrepreneurs all over the world. Knowledge becomes the only sustainable competitive advantage.

At least that's the general consensus.[2] I beg to differ from it in one respect.

Yes, the generation and use of knowledge will be the key to survival for an increasing number of companies, but the key to *success* will be the generation and use of *creative knowledge*. Knowledge is often no more than the rote and semirote learning of facts, concepts, and procedures. (If you read scholarly journals, you quickly learn that the few truly useful articles, the ones based on significant ideas and research, are virtually lost among the hundreds of articles that aren't.) I think that Peter Senge has it right: A successful organization must be "continually expanding its capacity to create its future."[3]

But how does an organization expand its capacity to create its future? By becoming and remaining more creative than its competitors.

Creativity is a broad, broad topic and, from an organization's point of view, a slightly scary one. Most authors and consultants who promote creativity assume that it's a good in itself, like multiple vitamins, and that organizations will automatically profit from an infusion of it. This book does *not* take that point of view. In fact, unfocused creativity may harm an organization more than it helps. What matters is not that creativity occurs, but that it constantly and directly supports the strategic goals of the organization. Successful creativity is *focused* creativity.

What Makes Creativity Valuable?

Suppose you were looking for a continually creative company—which one would you pick? Apple Computer might come to mind. For almost a decade now, Apple has been one of the most creative companies in the country. Suppose you could put Apple, or another constantly creative organization, under a microscope and examine its creativity "up close and personal." What would you find? You'd find that creativity is woven into the everyday operations of the company. And you'd find that this creativity permits the organization to constantly develop practices, processes, products, and services that are (1) new, (2) relevant to the organization's strategy, and (3) loaded with value for the organization, its customers, and its stakeholders. Let's examine each of these characteristics in more detail.

It's New

When a company is creative, it continually produces something *new*. *New* sounds great, and exciting, but we need to concentrate on its specific purpose. When an enterprise continually produces new practices, processes, products, and services, it maintains its competitive position vis-à-vis its competitors, *who cannot successfully anticipate what it will do.*

One of my favorite books is David Kearns and David Nadler's *Prophets in the Dark.** In it, David Kearns, the former CEO of Xerox, describes how he learned the importance of new ideas:

> When I was new at IBM, working in sales and taking a management training program in Sleepy Hollow, New York, I was rooming with a development engineer. One evening, I came back to my room grumbling about the lack of speed and reliability of the tape drives, and wondered why the engineers couldn't do something about it. My roommate stared at me with a look of total exasperation. "Boy, you guys in sales are all the same," he said. "You remind me of the farmer of 1850. If you asked him what he wanted, he would say he wanted a horse that was half as big and ate half as many oats and was twice as strong. And there would be no discussion of a tractor."[4]

In other words, it's never enough simply to envision tomorrow's product or service as a slightly improved adaptation of today's version. A creative company that intends to compete effectively must discover how to produce tomorrow's equivalent of tractors, not of more efficient horses. When it does this, it reaps one of the greatest competitive advantages a company can have: the ability to keep its competitors guessing.

It Fits the Strategy

If you regard creativity as good in itself, like motherhood, apple pie, and an extended-protection deodorant, it doesn't matter a lot whether what you create is relevant to the organization's strategy. Unfortunately, in the real world, companies live when they align what they do with their strategy, and die when they don't.

When you think of innovators, the commercial plastics in-

---

* Whenever a book is mentioned in the text, whether or not I've quoted from it, full information about the book appears in the Bibliography.

dustry doesn't jump to mind, yet Rubbermaid constantly creates new plastic products. Its managers have the same goal as the managers of 3M (known for its creativity for years): 25 percent of profits should come from products that did not exist five years ago.

Emerson Electric produces good, solid, low-cost consumer electronics and appliances. Its products aren't particularly innovative or cutting-edge; consumers get that from Sony or Masushita. But they are inexpensive, and they work. Emerson's expertise lies in its tight controls, limited product lines, and established technologies.

What would happen if you took Rubbermaid's genius for product innovation and grafted it onto Emerson Electric? Disaster, probably. Rapid product innovation and low-cost production just don't fit. As long as Emerson Electric attempts to be a low-cost provider, it may be creative, but its creativity won't be in cutting-edge products.[5]

Which is better, Rubbermaid's approach or Emerson Electric's? Neither, of course. Because they're pursuing different strategies; they apply creativity in different ways. Each is currently successful, and each will continue to be successful as long as it creates in ways that match its strategies. The fit between a company's strategy and its day-to-day operations is critical for its success. Corporations in hotly competitive markets must be creative, but their ability to focus their creativity on their strategy will determine their survival and their success.

It Creates Value

Every year, hundreds of new products and services are unleashed in the United States. Perhaps no other country in history has maintained such a high level of commercial and industrial creativity. Yet many of these products and services fail. Some fail because their projected users just don't get the benefit from them that justifies their cost. (I'd love to have a color laser printer, but I don't because its benefit to me falls far short of its cost.) Others fail even though users love them—because the company that produces them just can't make enough money from them to stay in business.

What's the common denominator? These products and services just don't produce enough value. For the last decade, we've concentrated on value to the customer. Certainly we should; after all, if the customer doesn't find value in a product or service, it's history. But that's not enough. The company too has to derive value from providing it. In short, the company must provide an affordable benefit to its customers *and at the same time* make enough money to keep itself in business.

That's hardly front-page news, so why bother saying it? If you want a genuinely creative organization, everyone in the organization has to understand why you need to create *both* kinds of value. Your personnel people have to understand that you can't adopt a snazzy new quality-of-work-life program unless it provides clear value to the organization. Your accountants must understand that dollars are a very limited way of tracking value, that very significant costs and values are off the balance sheet. For instance, you can't put an easy dollar value on the commitment of your players, but maintaining this commitment may very well be what keeps you in business. The people who produce your product or service need to understand the very real costs of customer dissatisfaction. And so on and so on.

It Produces New Practices, Processes, Products, and Services

Products can be seen, touched, and physically used. The advertising industry constantly calls our attention to new products. Most books on innovation focus on products. We see them in stores and on television, and use them at work and at home. They take up space. They can be tripped over, spilled, torn, and jammed. All this makes it easy to focus on new products and to think of a creative organization as one that produces these new products effectively.

That's only one side of the picture. For the other side, look for a moment at Toyota. Toyota is certainly one of the world's top automobile manufacturers. But how many product innovations has Toyota produced? Can you think of even one? I'm not downing the people at Toyota; they may have introduced a number of innovations in their cars (particularly in the Lexus line) that aren't obvious. But that's not why they're successful. Toyota rose to its present position as an automotive leader because of its innovations in the *processes* by which cars are made. Because of these process innovations, Toyota can build higher-quality cars, build them faster, and change over from one model to another faster than its competitors can. (If you still don't appreciate the impact of Toyota's process innovations, just read *The Machine That Changed the World*.)

Process creativity can be just as much of a competitive advantage as product or service creativity. In our focus on processes, though, we've overlooked *practices*.

What makes a practice different from a process? Processes have a mechanical ring to them. You process ore, or design processes to manufacture cars, or develop processes to record credit card transactions. Processes are often very precise repeated actions, whether done by a machine or by people; because of this, processes are relatively easy to chart, analyze, and improve.

Practices, on the other hand, are primarily social interactions among members of an organization. They're not so neat and tidy as processes, and may never be repeated just the same way twice. These three examples should help illustrate the difference:

1. The Ajax Corporation has a highly structured five-step process for making decisions. All managers are expected to use this process to make and defend their decisions. The practice, however, is for an individual manager to discuss an idea with several other managers until they reach a consensus, then use the process to explain and justify the decision.

2. There is a highly structured process that many organizations expect their course designers to use when developing training programs. In practice, experienced training designers often skip individual steps in the process and modify others in order to get the training produced rapidly. Their practice not only differs from the formal process but varies from one situation to another.

3. The practice of Uptown Banking is to work out detailed processes for branch tellers to follow for each different kind of transaction. In one branch, tellers seldom follow the formal process—because their practice is to get together for drinks every week or so and come up with ideas to expedite the processes.

Are processes and practices dramatically different from each other? No. They differ only in degree, and in one sense any process that involves people is part of a practice. But processes tend to be inflexible and spelled out in detail, while practices are more flexible, have more options, and are based on people interacting with one another.

Because they're based on human interaction, practices form a key part of any organization's operation, and a constantly creative organization exercises its creativity to improve its practices along with its processes. It looks at how people interact with one another and finds ways to make the interactions more effective. For instance, organizations find when they begin to use teams that successful teams must develop effective practices for dealing with internal conflict. A team may use specific processes for handling conflict, but its overall practices of how individuals treat one another when they differ will be at least as important as the specific processes—and deserve as much attention.

Creative organizations not only create new products; they create new processes and practices as well. And, finally, they create new services. In many ways, even for manufacturing firms, the services that a company provides are key to its success. AT&T's Business Systems Division makes and sells hardware systems to its customers, but the division has found that 90 percent of customer satisfaction depends on the services (before, during, and after the sale) that AT&T provides.[6] Acura builds a high-quality car, but its success has been based at least as much on the level of service it provides its customers. IBM was able to charge premium prices for its mainframes for years because of the high level of service it provided with its hardware.

Of course, many firms offer services as their primary "product." Financial services provide money management; the American Express Card looks like a product but is in fact a service. Cable TV provides a service, as does your barber, hairdresser, or astrologer. The list grows ever longer, particularly since in the United States and developed nations in general the percentage of organizations producing services has been rising sharply for many years. Even manufacturing enterprises typically have more players involved in providing internal and external services than in the manufacturing process itself.

Now we get to the most important point. Is it critical for you to clearly distinguish a process from a practice or to know to what extent you produce products as opposed to services? No, but it is critical to understand that a creative organization looks constantly both at *what* it produces (products and/or services) and at *how* it produces them (practices and processes). Sometimes one is more important, sometimes another. You may gain market share by coming up with a new product or service that fills a customer need (product or service creativity). You might gain even greater market share by providing your current product or service more quickly or with a higher level of quality or customization built in (practice or process creativity). Constantly creative organizations keep looking at every aspect of what they make and do to find directions that are new, aligned with the organization's strategy, and full of value for both the organization and its customers.

But How Can an Organization Be Constantly Creative?

With luck, I've piqued your interest by now. Perhaps you want to develop your organization into a constantly creative one. But isn't that an awfully tall order? How can you staff your organization with creative geniuses? And even if you could, how in the world could you get them to focus on the day-to-day work?

Our society does us a real disservice by identifying creativity with great "creative geniuses." When you think creativity, you probably think of da Vinci, Beethoven, Picasso, Einstein. Each of them, and hundreds of others, were truly creative geniuses. Not only do you and I not have their genius, but very, very few other "creative" people do either. That doesn't mean that these people or you or I aren't creative. They are, we are, and the people in organizations are—when the environment both requires and supports creativity.

The Saga of Dale and Ben

Let me give you an example of creativity where you might least expect it—on an automotive assembly line. Jobs on the line are carefully engineered, so each represents the appropriate set of tasks for one person. Certainly there's no room for creativity there. No? This is what Ben Hamper wrote in *Rivethead*, his book about life on the assembly line:

> Dale shared the same commitment I had to tryin' anything that would budge that minute hand in our favor. We quickly scrapped the hour on, hour off arrangement and went straight for the summit of the double-up system—a half day on, a half day off. This meant you could actually spend as little as four or five hours in the plant, get paid for the full time, and escape out of the chaos by sunset.
>
> This is how it worked: Dale and I would both report to work before the 4:30 horn. We'd spend a half hour preparing all the stock we would need for evening. At 5:00, I would take over the two jobs while Dale went to sleep in a makeshift cardboard bed behind our bench.
>
> I'd work the jobs from 5:00 until 9:24, the official Suburban/Blazer Line lunch period. When the line stopped, I'd give Dale's cardboard coffin a good kick and rouse him. . . . It was time for the handoff. I would give my ID badge to Dale so that he could punch me out at quitting time.
>
> Perfecting this kind of immaculate trickery called for complete reliability in one's partner. You had to be sure that the quality of the jobs remained faultless. You had to make extra certain to avoid any kind of injury. You had to refrain from all drinking.

Not a bad job—but it didn't end there. Ben and Dale got too cocky, and the supervisors decided to teach them a lesson. They assigned the two an additional task, a very awkward and unpredictable one.

> The bossmen motioned for Dale and me to come over. They explained how it would be. We would read the schedule taped to the front of each cab and this would inform us as to whether a certain truck called for

air-conditioning clamps. There would be no set pattern that we could rely on. . . . This kind of suspense was just what the bossmen were hoping would break up our system.

Attaching the air-conditioning clamp . . . wasn't a strenuous chore, it was more of an exasperation. You couldn't see the holes you were supposed to be screwing into. You had to feel around and, once you found them, you had to balance the air gun perfectly still so that the screw and clamp didn't vibrate off the miniature tip of the gun. If you missed your mark, everything would fly apart and you would be forced to start all over.

Did this lick our intrepid pair? Almost. Ben was about ready to admit defeat, but not Dale.

Dale wouldn't allow me to give up, assuring me that we'd be right back in business within a week.

And that unconcerned, soothsayin' pig farmer was right. Through determination, perspiration, acceleration and pure spite, we swallowed up the air-conditioning clamps into our routine and were back doubling-up within a week. We made for a helluva team. The neurotic, scam-happy city kid and the bullheaded, work-junkie farm boy.

Our return to glory didn't escape the notice of our supervisors. . . . As exasperated as they probably felt, they knew there was nothing they could really do to stop us. We showed up for work each and every day. We ran nothing but 100 percent defect-free quality. We kept our workplace spotless, provided you overlooked Dale's ugly slick of chewing tobacco juice. GM was very big on bottom lines and the bottom line as it pertained to Dale and me was that we were exemplary shoprats.[7]

In short, they reengineered their jobs, doubling productivity while keeping quality and safety high. And all this from two "shoprats" with no college and no creativity training.

The Seven Core Qualities of Creative Action

You don't find a creative genius like Frank Lloyd Wright or Albert Einstein every day, but you do find Dale and Ben and other "ordinary" people constantly doing creative things. And they display the same core qualities of creative action that Wright and Einstein did:

1. They intend to be creative.
2. They direct their creativity toward goals they care about.
3. They make high demands on themselves.
4. They focus on important problems, trying to find the opportunities within them.[8]
5. They spend a significant amount of time trying to formulate the problem in depth before attempting to solve it.
6. They consider a wide variety of alternatives before committing themselves to a specific direction.
7. They often make many attempts, none of them quite satisfactory, before they come up with the right solution.

(Just for the record, Dale and Ben clearly had all these qualities except number 5. The account doesn't tell whether they spent time formulating the problem in depth.)

A constantly creative organization looks for players with more creative potential than the players in other organizations possess, but it thrives by developing the innate creativity of everyone. And it accomplishes this, first and foremost, by developing the seven core qualities and then building these seven qualities into everyone's job. This suggests that we should look at the core qualities in somewhat greater detail.[9]

1. *Creative organzations intend to be creative.* Does this sound obvious to the point of being silly? It's not. Stop and think how often you've read that companies must send people to "creativity" training, teach them special "creative" skills, and use special "creative" methods like brainstorming if they want their people to be creative. Each of these techniques has its place, but individually or all together they do not make an enterprise creative. Companies are creative, first and foremost, because they *intend*

to be creative and they expect their players to be creative. It takes a lot more, but it begins here.

2. *Creative organizations expect their members to direct their creativity toward goals that are important to the organization.* I can't emphasize this too much. Creative people in traditional organizations often direct their attention to what's interesting to them—with little concern for how important it is to the organization. That's why traditional organizations are often so edgy about hiring creative people except in certain, specific "creative" departments (like R&D or package design).

The cure, of course, isn't to banish creativity to a small corner of the organization. Instead, companies that intend to compete in today's fast-changing markets make sure that everyone knows and understands the strategic goals of the firm and how they apply to each individual, each team, and each department. High-performance organizations differ from traditional organizations perhaps more on this quality than any other: They ensure that everyone knows where the organization is heading so that they can direct their best energies toward getting there.[10]

I came on a striking example of this a few months ago. Horst Schultze is the CEO of the Ritz-Carlton chain, the top-rated hotel chain in the world from 1987 through 1991 (and second in 1992). In the course of a magazine interview, he emphasized the importance of employees and the chain's concern for its employees. The interviewer pooh-poohed what he said as just another stack of PR verbiage from a large corporation. Schultze immediately asked that one of the dishwashers be sent up from the kitchen. In a minute, a young man named Steve appeared, and Schultze asked him how he was involved in the hotel's operation over and above his specific job. "Well," Steve said, "we've just finished our strategic plan. . . ." *That's* what it means for everyone to understand the strategic goals of the enterprise.[11]

3. *Creative organizations expect their members to perform at a very high level.* We know now beyond any question that exceptional organizations of all kinds expect continuing high levels of performance from all their players. For instance, we often think that successful teams are those that have been carefully trained in team building and other team skills. Many times they are, but as

Jon Katzenbach and Douglas Smith stress again and again in *The Wisdom of Teams*, high performance expectations are consistently the best predictors of team success.[12]

A creative organization is by definition a high-performance organization. If it begins to settle for less than consistently excellent performance, it ceases to challenge its best people. If you think it's difficult to win back lost customers, try relighting the spark under someone who was once creative but hasn't been challenged for months or years. Of course, you may not have to; the odds are that she will find an organization that offers a meaningful challenge and simply leave you.

4. *Creative organizations expect their members to focus on important problems.* The goal of a traditional organization is to have as few problems as possible and to routinize the few that it has. Creative organizations orient themselves 180 degrees away from this approach. They *seek out* problems, or, to be more exact, they seek the *opportunities* that are hiding in problems. The best companies constantly attempt to find what their customers want that they can't yet provide and then to find a way to provide it. They attack problems like this with gusto, looking for the significant opportunities and confident that they can find the solution. Developing a computer that users can operate intuitively, without having to become computer-literate, is an extraordinarily difficult problem. But Apple Computer has devoted itself to this goal single-mindedly—and built a worldwide business in the process.

Note something: A creative organization is never merely solving problems, spending its efforts on getting an irritating situation to go away. It searches for the *opportunities* in the problems and then solves the problems by seizing the opportunities. Apple doesn't just try to overcome the problem of "user hostility" to computers; it strives to create computers that enable people to carry out tasks with less effort and greater effectiveness than they could before. In fact, Apple's Newton MessagePad is just one more step toward its goal of lodging computing ability in friendly devices that neither look nor feel like computers. Apple is attempting to create not an improved computer but an entirely new kind of computer; this goal is what sets it apart from most of its competitors.

Focusing on important problems and turning them into opportunities require two critical skills. First, a creative organization must see that its members become very good at converting *conditions* into *problems*. A condition is something that can't be altered; death and taxes are the most famous of these. A problem is something that can be changed; it has a solution. Really creative organizations have the ability to take what other organizations regard as fixed conditions, convert them into problems, and then solve them.

Second, a creative organization ensures that its members have highly developed critical abilities, so that early in the process they can weed out mediocre ideas or ideas that are too fixated on problems rather than opportunities. When you read about creativity, critical ability often comes out the bad guy: Turn off your critical faculties if you want to be creative. If you're just beginning to develop your creativity, or if an idea is in the first, tender stages, that's good advice. Once you become proficient, however, you'll get stuck in comfortable mediocrity unless you develop and use your critical abilities. And organizations can get just as stuck. How can it know which problems are important, which opportunities are most promising, unless it can think about them and evaluate them effectively? Creativity first, yes—but then cold, hard thought.

5. *Creative organizations expect their members to spend a significant amount of time trying to formulate a problem in depth before attempting to solve it.* Many problems that organizations confront are *structured* problems. They involve one area and can be solved with relative ease by someone experienced in that area. If the college recruiting program is lapsing, a good recruiting specialist can build it back up without spending weeks or months analyzing it. Unfortunately, the significant problems are all *unstructured*. They often appear first to an organization as *messes*, which is the more familiar name for a complex problem that cannot be solved simply by applying experience from one function. Customer dissatisfaction with the quality of a service, for instance, can seldom be resolved in any single department.

A creative firm realizes that many seemingly structured problems are actually unstructured problems in disguise. The college recruiting problem may result from the company's sinking reputation as an employer, or from the perception that its products or services are substandard, or from a change in the goals of graduating students—or from a combination of all three factors.

When a company rushes to define a problem, it typically picks the most familiar form of the problem and attacks it. Want to beef up college recruiting? Hire three more recruiters, and let's get on with it. Creative companies act otherwise. When they have a mess, or a simple-appearing problem that may actually conceal a mess, they take the time to examine it.

Ross Perot once complained that whenever GM found a snake its response was to appoint a snake committee to analyze the snake and make recommendations. He contrasted this with EDS's approach: The first person who sees the snake kills it. A creative organization does neither habitually. It looks the snake over carefully, perhaps pokes it once or twice, and then chooses the proper response—which may be to cage it and sell it to someone.[13]

6. *Creative organizations expect their members to consider a wide variety of alternatives before committing themselves to a specific direction.* Research makes it clear that considering a wide range of alternatives has more effect on the quality and creativity of a final decision than almost any other single factor. We all tend to make decisions quickly, particularly when confronted by a pressing problem. As a result, we limit ourselves to just a few, comfortable alternatives and then choose among them. At best, this yields limited results. At worst, it creates a "solution" worse than the original problem.

7. *Creative organizations know that their members must often make many attempts, none of them quite satisfactory, before they come up with the "right" solution.* Occasionally "instant creativity" happens. John Philip Sousa claimed that his famous *Stars and Stripes* march came to him in its entirety as he was returning to the United States from a trip abroad. I don't doubt him, but this wasn't the way he normally composed—nor is it the way that an organization should expect creativity to occur. Ideas don't pop up from the ground fully mature any more than apples or oak trees do.

Any individual or organization intending to be creative must realize that ideas will take time to mature. Frederick W. Taylor, the founder of Scientific Management, and his associates confronted early on the complex calculations involved in machining a piece of metal. They invented a slide rule that made these calculations almost automatic, a tremendously creative accomplishment—but it took them *eighteen years* and any number of false starts to do it. With luck, you won't have to wait that long for a specific idea to mature, but it won't often mature in eighteen hours either. You can get a quick solution or you can get a creative solution, but you cannot reliably get both together.

What to Do Now

You probably have some sense now of how your organization stacks up as a creative organization, at least on the seven core qualities. But I want to help you to get an even clearer picture. What follows are summaries of the seven qualities combined with a simple rating scale. For each quality, mark an X on the line, rating your organization from 0 (if the quality is completely untrue of it) to 10 (if the quality is completely true of it). When you finish rating it on all seven core qualities, draw a line connecting each of the ratings; this will give you a snapshot of how your organization looks at present.

The ratings aren't designed simply to help you rate your organization; they have a more practical purpose than that. You can't change your organization overnight, but you can begin to work on one or two of the core qualities. The chapter ends with specific suggestions for moving toward a more creative organization. Pick the one or two qualities that you most want to work on and start applying the suggestions. This will start you moving in the right direction. The more you move, and the more consistently you move, the easier it becomes to move further.

The Seven Core Qualities of a Creative Organization

1. My organization intends to be creative, and
   its members are creative.   0———5———10

2. The members of my organization direct their
   creativity toward goals that are important to
   the organization.   0———5———10

3. The members of my organization perform at
a very high level.   0———5———10

4. My organization is good at identifying important problems and finding the opportunities within them.   0———5———10

5. My organization takes time to formulate a problem in depth before deciding how to solve it.   0———5———10

6. My organization considers a wide variety of alternatives before committing itself to a specific direction.   0———5———10

7. My organization often has to make frequent attempts, none of them quite satisfactory, before it comes up with the right solution.   0———5———10

Now that you've created a quick visual profile of your current organization, you can choose where to begin changing it. For each of the seven core qualities listed there is a corresponding suggestion. After you've thought about the qualities and read the seven suggestions, choose one or two suggestions to begin implementing tomorrow morning. Don't expect instant success. Do expect progress, an occasional setback, and an occasional breakthrough. Don't let the setbacks stop you, and see that the organization celebrates every breakthrough.

1. *Does your organization lack creative intent?* You could simply call everyone together tomorrow morning and announce that henceforth the organization will be creative. But there's a much more effective way to begin with this characteristic, and I can't do better than to quote Larry Farrell's *Searching for the Spirit of Enterprise*:

> The best definition of innovation is the broadest. Everyone should come to work determined to do something, anything, better each day. . . . Every shred of research into the process of innovation says the same thing: The way to innovate is to try something, anything, again, again, and again. . . . Maintaining the business, which

most people are programmed to do, is really losing the business. Growing and prospering demand that all of us do something, anything, better each day.[14]

There you have it in a nutshell. For the next ninety days at least, preach this. Live it yourself. Expect it. You may be surprised at the results of something so simple.

2. *Are the members of your organization not directing their creativity toward goals that are important to the organization?* Start by ensuring that the goals are widely communicated, widely understood, and intelligently pursued (remember Horst Schultze and the Ritz Carlton). Any number of books or consultants can help you accomplish this. Even if your organization never becomes a constantly creative one, this one step will almost certainly improve its performance.

3. *Are the members of your organization not performing at a consistently high level?* You know that this is a problem in itself. Organizations get high performance from their members when they combine clear, worthwhile goals with individual autonomy to accomplish them. You may be trying to manage your organization by telling individuals not only what to do but *how* to do it. You can begin scaling back this overcontrol immediately, though it may take several months to convince people you really mean it. Begin with effective delegation. If you're not sure how to accomplish this successfully, read William Oncken's *Managing Management Time* or my own *New Manager's Survival Manual*.

You may also want to ask yourself whether individuals and teams in your organization really get rewarded for high performance. Don't just look at the formal compensation plan and recognition program. Look at who gets promoted, who gets the best assignments, who's thought to have a good "track record." Are they high performers, or simply solid, competent performers who don't take risks and therefore don't make mistakes? You probably should ask yourself this question at least once a year, just on general principles.

4. *Are the members of your organization unskilled at identifying important problems and then finding the opportunities within them?* If

your organization doesn't practice effective delegation based on clear goals and the individual freedom to accomplish them, few individuals will develop effective problem-solving and opportunity-finding skills. High performance and effective problem solving go hand in hand; work on one effectively and the other will begin to improve along with it. Training can help, because many problem-solving techniques (such as the eight basic techniques taught as part of TQM) can be learned quickly and effectively. But don't count on training alone to solve the problem. It won't. And don't let preoccupation with problems overshadow the search for the opportunities within them.

5. *Does your organization fail to take time to formulate a problem in depth before deciding how to solve it?* The odds are that everyone is under pressure to produce, and produce quickly. Spending the time required to explore a problem deeply may be looked on as waste. If that's the problem, you can't change it overnight. Pick an important problem or two and assign them to a task force. (If you already have multifunctional teams, so much the better; give them the problems.) Make it clear that you intend for them to evaluate the problem in depth, then provide you with the results of their analysis. Insist that they do exactly this.

6. *Do the members of your organization fail to consider a wide variety of alternatives before committing themselves to a specific direction?* Both the cause and the cure are similar to number 5; in fact, they're almost a matched pair. Follow the same path. Make generating a broad range of alternatives one of the major objectives. Then ensure that the group meets the objective before you accept its results.

There may be another reason why your organization doesn't consider a broad range of alternatives. You may be defining problems within such a narrow frame of reference that you automatically exclude many promising alternatives. Chapter 3 deals with this problem in detail and suggests ways to organize to overcome it.

7. *Do the members of your organization consistently look for quick, one-shot solutions to problems?* Organizations that fail to search for multiple alternatives often settle for finding and implementing the "right" solution the first time around. This seldom works;

instead, it virtually guarantees that the organization will lock onto routine, *non*creative solutions.

It takes a while for an organization to accept that more effective solutions require experimentation; it has to experiment with the approach itself before it can have confidence in it. In essence, the organization must find a process that enables it to bite off real but manageable problems, attack the problems with limited resources, solve them, and then build on the results it gets. (Robert Schaffer's book *The Breakthrough Strategy* presents one effective way to do this.) The key is a clear and easily understood method that can be learned and applied rapidly and that will help the organization to repeat many problem-solving cycles in a short period of time.

Chapter 2

How Is an Organization a Creative System?

I believe the one rule that is definite and applies to everyone is that you need sweat and pain and a lot of hard work, and then it has to appear effortless.

I remember reading something Ginger Rogers said once in the *New York Times* when they were doing a salute to Fred Astaire. She said that at many rehearsals their feet would bleed. Remember how easy it looked? That's high artistry.

—Tony Bennett

How do you tell when someone has truly mastered a skill? When he or she performs so well and so effortlessly that excellence becomes "nothing special." Similarly, in a well-known Zen account, a Zen master asked about the essence of Zen replies, "Nothing special." And if you ask someone in a constantly creative organization what he or she does to be so creative, the answer might also be "Nothing special." In a creative organization, creativity is such an ingrained way of life that it becomes just the way that business is done. An organization has not become truly creative until its creativity becomes simply its everyday way of doing what it does.

How can this happen? Most simply put, an organization practices creativity as nothing special when it becomes a *creative system*. Not just a collection of creative individuals, but creative in its totality—a creative system. Nothing else will substitute for a creative system. This chapter explains how an organization can become such a creative system.

I blew hot and cold on systems theory for almost two decades. Then, two years ago, I attended a workshop that used organizational systems as its basis. The way the workshop used systems turned me off completely—but then a strange thing happened. I was so irritated by the approach that I began scribbling systems diagrams and shuffling their little boxes around on my own. A series of "aha!" moments followed. The eventual result was a systems model that actually helps people understand and develop organizational systems, particularly creative organizational systems.

When you look at a traditional systems diagram, what you see is *inputs* being neatly transformed by *processes* into *outputs*, sometimes with a feedback loop running from the output box to the input box. Figure 2-1 presents such a traditional systems diagram.

I can all but promise you that if you take this kind of systems diagram and try to make sense of your organization with it—well, you might as well do it on a Caribbean cruise so that you'll at least get something out of the effort. Systems do have processes. However, they have many different kinds of results or outcomes, and only some of these are the intended outputs. Calling what goes into systems "inputs" may work for limited manufacturing or data systems, but it doesn't work very well with organizations. And the feedback loop shown on a conventional chart is most misleading of all.

Let me propose a very different kind of systems model. For $I \to P \to O$ (input-process-output), let's substitute $D \to O \to R/F^2$ (drivers → operations → results/modified by feedback). $D \to O \to R/F^2$ may seem strange, but what it stands for can help materially

Figure 2-1. The traditional systems diagram.

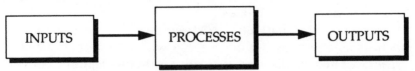

to explain organizations in general and creative organizations in particular.

What an Organizational System Does

First and foremost, an organization is a system that attempts to transform decisions about *customer requirements* into *actual customer benefits*. This definition accurately summarizes both the economic and the social function of an organization. To expand it to encompass what really happens in the organization, however, we must substitute more inclusive terms: *drivers* for requirements, *operations* for processes, and *results* for benefits. You'll see why in a few paragraphs. Figure 2-2 is the core of an organizational systems model based on the definition.

Even in so simple a form, the model is more useful than a traditional diagram. It captures the essential function of an organizational system—to turn requirements into results that will benefit someone outside the system. But we can easily expand the model, and each expansion makes it more and more helpful.

Results (Outputs, Waste, Surprises, Invisible Consequences)

First, we need to look much more intently at the results of a real system. Every system is designed to produce certain outputs, and these outputs are all that show as results in the traditional model. However, they are not *all* of the results. A system produces four very different kinds of results, and each result is important in its own right. Figure 2-3 expands the "RESULTS"

Figure 2-2.　The revised systems model, stage 1.

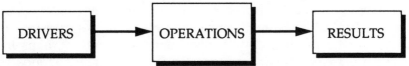

Figure 2-3.   The revised systems model, stage 2.

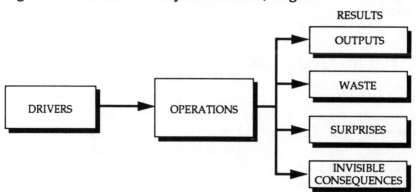

block into these four kinds of results. Here's a quick look at each
of the four:

1. *Outputs.* Every system is designed to produce certain
outputs. Not surprisingly, everyone tends to focus on these
outputs. Surprisingly, in some cases they constitute the least
noteworthy result of the system.

2. *Waste.* As the quality movement made us realize, waste
forms another major class of results. Waste is a product or service
that was intended as an output but that cannot be used as
produced. A training course that fails to develop the intended
level of performance is waste, as is a long-distance call directed to
the wrong number. The greater the waste, the less efficient the
system is. If you're familiar with quality terminology, you've
noted that my definition of waste includes both scrap and rework.
When a system produces an unusable output, it has failed,
whether or not the output can be transformed later into something usable.

3. *Surprises.* All systems create surprises, either pleasant or
unpleasant. A difficult new inventory system may result in a
surprisingly higher turnover among inventory clerks. New software using artificial intelligence may result in a surprising increase in the productivity of investment advisers—perhaps because it increases their confidence in their recommendations. A

section may automate a particular report, saving time for itself but, as it finds out later, making the report harder for its customers to interpret.

Surprise becomes particularly important when a system is changed. The greater the change, the greater the probability of unintended consequences. As Isaac Asimov succinctly put it in his final science-fiction novel:

> You must have minimalism because every change, any change, has a myriad of side effects that can't always be allowed for. If the change is too great and the side effects too many, then it becomes certain that the outcome will be far removed from anything you've planned and that it would be entirely unpredictable.[1]

Because the effects of change become more unpredictable the larger the change, when large-scale change occurs unintended consequences may well be more significant than the planned ones. It's helpful to keep this in mind when designing and implementing change, and particularly when you're confronted with recommendations to create "transformational" change.

4. *Invisible Consequences.* Finally, all systems produce invisible consequences. The results (like the Emperor's new clothes) aren't invisible in any absolute sense; someone from outside the organization observing the system's operation might notice the results at once. But the leaders of the organization don't see them—either because they aren't looking for them or because the results would be too inconvenient if they became visible. The rigid organization of the American automakers' assembly lines produced a level of worker alienation and resentment that didn't become fully visible until the Japanese were able to organize similar operations in a way that noticeably reduced this negative impact.

Results in a Creative Organizational System

Focusing on all four results rather than simply on outputs makes us more realistic about what systems actually do and far more prepared for the impact of changes on these systems. But such a focus can accomplish even more for us. Traditional organizational systems concentrate on outputs, attempt to banish waste and surprise, and overlook invisible consequences. Creative organizational systems differ in almost every way, but two of their characteristics are especially important for our purposes. First, they treat the relationship between outputs and waste in a very specific way. Second, they spend significant time examining waste and surprises and attempting to surface invisible consequences—all in search of new opportunities.

Separating the Wheat From the Chaff

A constantly creative organization attempts to minimize waste, of course, but it takes care to determine just what waste really is. The quality movement first called the problem of waste to our attention. For that movement, waste has a very clear and specific meaning: Waste is any product that fails to meet the requirements of the system. This definition works, however, only if you already know for sure exactly what the desired outputs are, if you can clearly tell the wheat from the chaff.

What happens when the organizational system is creating outputs that aren't defined and that can't even be known for sure until they've been created? The answer: You don't know what's waste until the outputs have been created and examined.

I don't want this one to slip by you, so let me repeat it: You don't know what's waste until the outputs have been created and examined.

This understanding of waste differs significantly from the conventional one. As I stressed in Chapter 1, a creative organization spends noticeable time on activities that a traditional organization considers waste. A creative organization not only permits but expects its members to spend a significant amount of time trying to formulate a problem in depth before attempting to solve it; it expects its members to consider a wide variety of alternatives before committing themselves to a specific direction; and it knows that its members must often make many attempts, none of them quite satisfactory, until they come up with the "right" solution. Consider these waste, as a traditional company would, and you've gutted the creative organization.

Make no mistake, though, a creative organization does look at the "wasted" time and effort to see what it can learn. Can the product or service be produced with less time and effort next time? Can some of the ideas developed in the process be saved for future use, or perhaps even used for a different client? This helps improve operations, and it creates an occasion for even broader learning.

Before turning to the second characteristics of creative organizational systems where results are concerned, let me raise—and answer—one question: You must spend time formulating problems, considering alternatives, and experimenting with solutions, but how can you tell when these activities have stopped being productive and become a form of waste? Here's a useful rule of thumb:

> Activities that support creativity become waste when they begin to retrace previous steps without adding anything new or when they focus on marginal changes (ultimately the same thing).

Do members keep formulating the problem in the same ways, offering only minor variations on previous alternatives and contributing nothing more than "tweaks" to the final solution? When this happens, it's time to move on, either to the next step or to a deeper level of the problem. (I explain this more fully in Chapter 6.)

Now, on to the second aspect.

Digging Into the Trash

The second characteristic of creative organizational systems is this: They pore over waste, surprises, and invisible consequences with a passion in an attempt to spot new opportunities. Effort spent that failed to contribute to a successful output or that brought about a result no one expected may point to an unrecognized opportunity.[2] And because a creative organization is always trying to loosen its frames (as I point out in Chapter 3), it constantly searches for consequences that aren't visible at first glance.

Thus, a creative organization not only treats waste in a way different from that of a traditional organizational system, but it also uses waste, surprise, and invisible consequences as a source of opportunity. These are the first two structural characteristics of a creative organizational system, and they both describe how it treats the results of its operations. Now we need to examine how a system produces its results.

Operations (Practices, Processes, Constraints, and Resources)

Both the traditional and the revised systems models agree on this point: Something happens within a system that produces a significant change. The traditional model makes processes the key to transforming inputs into outputs. In Chapter 1, I suggested that practices are as important to a creative organization as processes, so that both practices and processes are required to transform requirements into results.

Processes, with or without practices, are just the tip of the iceberg in the operation of an organizational system. In the traditional picture of systems, processes stand in lonely isolation, linking inputs to outputs. But processes (and practices) never operate in isolation. All real-world processes and practices consume *resources* and operate within *constraints*, and you cannot understand a practice or process fully until you understand both the resources it consumes and the constraints under which it operates. Figure 2-4 adds these to the model.

All systems consume resources to accomplish their results. Some of the resources are obvious. Manufacturing systems consume raw materials. Reserach and development consumes the time of scientists and engineers. But the resources required by the processes and practices of an organizational system run much deeper. They include:

- Wear and tear on and obsolescence of the technology involved

Figure 2-4. The revised systems model, stage 3.

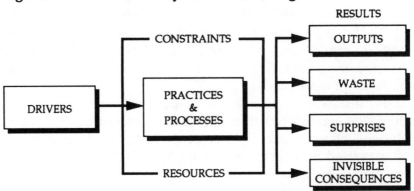

- The skills and motivation of the people who make the system function
- Ideas that help it function more efficiently
- Any other physical, mental, or emotional resource that contributes directly to the functioning of the system

Some of the resources consumed by a process, like ideas and (happily) creativity in a variety of forms, are renewable. Many, such as raw materials, supplies, and time, are not. This suggests a useful rule of thumb:

> The more that the resources consumed by the processes of a system are renewable resources, the more productive the system will be over the long run.

If this is the case, a system that draws heavily on creativity will be extremely productive and efficient. Think about it.

All systems also operate under constraints, and all constraints share two important characteristics:

1. *They're external to the practices and processes they constrain.* The constraints may be external to the organization as a whole, such as government laws and regulations. They may also be

internal to the organization, such as the organization's policies and procedures or any labor agreement it may have.

2. *The system doesn't require the constraints to accomplish its results.* In other words, they aren't part of the requirements that constitute the system. They do not help the system function more effectively or more efficiently.

For instance, an organization may provide computer systems integration services to various customers. The organization's results will have to take account of the different hardware and software used by a customer, the customer's degree of networking, and similar factors. These are not constraints; they are characteristics of effective results and are part of the requirements. However, if the organization's policy prevents technicians from physically modifying a system unless an engineer is present, that is a constraint.

From an operating point of view, resources help practices and processes accomplish their purposes, while constraints hinder these practices and processes. This is not a value judgment on the validity of any constraint or on constraints in general; it's simply a factual statement about the impact of constraints. From the point of view of those operating the system, resources are desirable and constraints irritating. From the point of view of higher levels in the organization (higher-level systems), the reverse may well be the case. In fact, higher levels of the system often impose constraints whose specific purpose is to limit the resources that a system can consume.

Constraints and Resources in a Creative Organizational System

The people who operate the processes and perform the practices in a traditional organization experience constraints (or controls) that unreasonably limit their access to the resources they need. They experience this because in hierarchies of any size the concern with controlling access to resources begins to overwhelm the concern that the resources be available. New hires must be approved three levels up; supplies can only be requisitioned every other week; capital expenditures over $500 must be approved at the VP level, and so on and on and on.

If the system is meeting stable requirements with stable outputs, it can often tolerate the delay this control causes. But as soon as requirements and results begin to change, the delay begins to matter. When change becomes as constant as it is today, the delays become critical. Either the constraints are loosened or the system begins to fail.

Unfortunately, even the most stable system has a high invisible overhead, one that constitutes a major cost of (non)quality in the organization. The overhead consists of all the time and effort spent getting around the controls and to the resources. This cost, which has only recently begun to be recognized for what it is, makes up one of the major invisible consequences of the controls and constitutes a major source of waste.

A truly bureaucratic organization, however, takes one more step: It gives responsibility for constraints to the organizations created to provide the resources. The human resources department not only fills jobs but enforces the organization's hiring, EEO, and safety policies. Information services not only provides computer support but tightly regulates the use of personal computers. This arrangement virtually guarantees that the resourcing process will be subordinate to the control process, and that the time spent getting around the constraints will skyrocket. In my own opinion, it is a basic flaw in traditional bureaucracies—whether these are in the private sector or the public sector.[3]

The point? If anything I've said so far has been obvious, it should be that a creative organization must escape this trap. It can do this in only one way: It must (1) make those operating the system responsible for controlling it and (2) then provide them with free access to the resources they need.

Both these requirements sound scary to any traditional manager—and even to me. But both must happen. Fortunately, we know something about how to accomplish them. The whole idea of empowering individual performers means, very specifically, moving from formal organizational controls to control by individual, team, and unit self-management based on shared values and goals. When an organization accomplishes this, it can dismantle much of the control structure. Then it can convert what remains of this structure into a means for creating and communicating goals, developing mutually agreed-upon standards, and providing feedback to members.

An organization can accomplish much of this in another way. If the resources required by a system can be accurately priced, the organization simply lets the price mechanism control how many of what resources get used. The best way I know of to ensure the accuracy of prices is to let those who operate the system buy their resources wherever they can obtain the greatest value—internally or externally. We certainly know by now that the free market is the best guarantor of value.

(Don't think that I'm just peddling pipe dreams. My group, which operates as part of the largest functioning bureaucracy in the United States, has sold its services to internal customers for several years now. This is no internal bookkeeping exercise; all our customers are free to procure what we sell anywhere else if they can get better value there. Needless to say, we work very hard to ensure that they never do!)

Drivers (Goals, Objectives, Requirements, and Procedures)

So far we have talked as though organizational systems were driven exclusively by requirements, a serious oversimplification. Organizations do have requirements, and objectives and procedures as well. All of these, however, flow from the *goals* of the organization. Someone somewhere in the organization must decide what customers to serve with the products and/or to provide with the services. These decisions create the basic goals of the organization, and all its objectives, requirements, and procedures flow from these goals. Figure 2-5 presents this revised version of the model.

Virtually all organizations expand their goals into objectives, requirements, and procedures. An organizational system may thus be driven by any of the four, in any combination. How the system performs, though, depends on the way it uses these drivers as surely as the performance of an automobile depends on the engine that powers it.

Figure 2-5.   The revised systems model, stage 4.

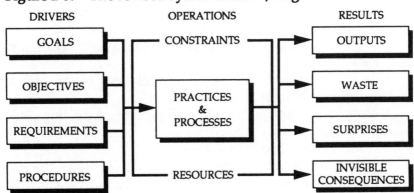

Let's look very briefly at the characteristics of each type of driver:

- *Goals* are broad expressions of organizational intent. Organizations move toward their goals, but often cannot precisely measure their progress in attaining them. Goals provide no guidance on how they are to be achieved and can normally be accomplished in a variety of ways.
- *Objectives* are more precise statements of organizational intent. They are normally measurable and time-bound. Although they define the area for action, they do not provide detailed guidance on what to do. They are more precise about what is to be done, but leave some room for choosing how to do it.
- *Requirements* are very specific outcomes that can be both measured and clearly defined. When Philip Crosby defined quality as conformance to requirements, he intended this meaning. Requirements are very precise about what is to be done and normally have precise ways (processes) of accomplishing the outcomes associated with them.
- *Procedures* are the specific steps to be taken to produce an outcome. A procedure will ordinarily (but not always) state what the goal is, but concentrates on how to accomplish it. A system driven by procedures, as many bureaucracies are, defines effectiveness as adherence to the procedures.

Here is a short example of the differences among the four drivers:

- The division will return to profitability within six months (*Goal*).
- Each department will reduce overall costs by at least 15 percent within ninety days (*Objective*).
- Each department will abolish 75 percent of existing clerk-typist jobs and will reduce its word-processing staff by 30 percent within sixty days (*Requirement*).
- Each department will follow the requirements of the personnel policy manual to determine which individuals to let go (*Procedure*).

Goals, objectives, requirements, and procedures do not necessarily conflict with one another; all four can be used simultaneously. Indeed, most organizational systems require all four. In particular, goals and objectives require each other. Lieutenant General William Pagonis expresses this relationship succinctly:

> In my terminology, a goal is something that is nonquantifiable, purposely broad, and overarching. Once everyone in the organization understands the goals of the organization, then each person sets out several objectives by which to attain those goals at that given time, within his or her own sphere of activity.[4]

He might have gone on to add that at some point these goals and objectives become requirements and that the requirements may well generate the procedures needed to accomplish them. However, objectives are more restrictive than goals, requirements more restrictive than objectives, and procedures almost completely restrictive.

Goals and Objectives in a Creative Organizational System

We should draw a simple and straightforward lesson from this part of the organizational systems model: Each individual in a creative organization needs to understand and work toward goals and objectives, even if he must meet specific requirements and follow specific procedures.

In a traditional, hierarchical organization, goals belong to the executive level, objectives to the functional level, and the working level is left with requirements and procedures. In theory, this works fine. In reality, if the organization is of any size at all, requirements can get seriously out of sync with the goals and remain so. This can happen either when the organization lacks clear goals or when circumstances are changing (or both, of course).

If we take this lesson seriously, it means that no individual in a creative organization can ever work solely to meet requirements, much less just to follow procedures. Like Steve at the Ritz-Carlton, each player works to achieve the overall goals of the organization and to meet specific objectives that support those goals. He or she may also have very specific requirements to meet and procedures to follow, but these must never replace or overwhelm the goals and objectives.

The "why" of this is simple. In Chapter 1, I pointed out that creative organizations must be high-performing organizations, and that individuals commit themselves to high-level performance only when they are meeting goals and objectives meaningful to them. Thirty years of organizational research makes this fact clear: When performers are constrained by requirements and procedures divorced from broader objectives and goals, they simply do what is expected of them, no more. Since no creative organization can afford this level of performance, the organization ensures that every performer understands and works toward clear and meaningful goals and objectives.

A final point for this section. You've often heard that individuals are more likely to commit themselves to objectives that they have had a hand in developing. I'm not going to belabor this point here. Because management writings have emphasized the importance of mutually set objectives for promoting "ownership" of objectives, however, we've tended to overlook the communication advantages of mutually set objectives. Studies over the past three decades have shown again and again that one-way communication (I talk and you listen and perhaps ask questions) is an unreliable way to establish a common understanding. Effective managers often spend time with their performers, checking to ensure that they both agree on what should be done and what the priorities are. This helps, but it often helps as much and is certainly more efficient to spend the time up front, working with the performers to develop objectives that are mutually agreed-upon *and mutually understood* from the beginning.

F^2 (Tactical and Strategic Feedback)

All individuals and systems must have some form of feedback if they are to manage their own performance. They may or may not get this feedback. Performers (including managers) typically find that their basic feedback is: If no one is chewing on you, things must be going OK. Many organizations attempt to operate with about the same level of external feedback: If customers aren't complaining too loudly, everything must be going OK.

Needless to say, feedback doesn't get any more primitive than this. Such feedback will generally keep an individual or organization going at the same level of proficiency in a stable situation. Just as soon as the race speeds up, however, this Model T feedback will get its user run off the road in a flash.

In fact, an organization requires not one but two different forms of feedback to function effectively. The first is *tactical* feedback, which tells the company whether it's doing things right. The second is *strategic* feedback; it tells the organization whether it's doing the right thing. Notice the relationship between the two forms of feedback and the two forms of quality. Figure 2-6 adds both feedback loops to the model.

Although both types of feedback are genuine feedback, each serves quite a different purpose, and the organization must use each in a different way:

• *Tactical feedback* needs to come directly to the operations that are producing the results. It may come from internal sources, answering questions like: How many defects are we producing? How much time is there until the next deliverables are due? What changes does the operations manual require for it to be accurate? It may also come from external sources, that is, from the cus-

Figure 2-6. The complete revised systems model.

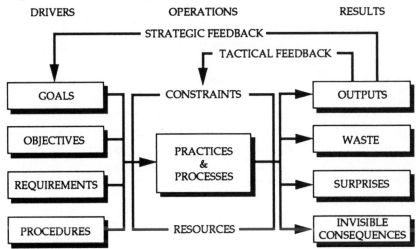

tomer. How satisfied are customers with our products or services? How willing is the customer to buy from us again? This feedback tells the system how well it's meeting the identified requirements of its customers.

• *Strategic feedback* may come from any source, but will normally come from customers (internal or external), competitors, or other parts of the environment. It answers much broader and less specific questions: Are we delivering the right products or services? Are we producing the benefits to the customer that we intended? Are our strategic goals appropriate to the market? The answers tell the system not how well it's meeting requirements but whether it's identifying the right requirements.

Neither type of feedback will substitute for the other. The organization may be providing high-quality, on-time services at a reasonable price—to a market that wants less and less of this type of service. Tactical feedback will not relay this information. Or the organization may shift its product line to be more in tune with the market, but be unable to deliver the products in sufficient quantity or with acceptable quality. Strategic feedback will not tell it that this is the case until too late. All organizations need both forms of feedback to succeed.[5]

F² in a Creative Organizational System

Traditional organizations typically have deficient feedback systems. For all but the most routine operations, and even sometimes for them, feedback on an operation comes not to the performers but to managers one, two, or even three levels above them. Such tactical feedback as exists is usually highly summarized and seldom available in time to correct current operations. Such strategic feedback as exists is channeled through a few specialized departments, primarily marketing; if it points to significant differences between the organization's products and the market's needs, it may take months or even years to influence organizational goals.

Organizations that successfully adopt a TQM culture make major improvements in this situation. At the operating level, they establish feedback systems that provide results to performers in time for them to make necessary changes quickly. They emphasize "listening to the voice of the customer," and many of them regularly dispatch performers to talk to customers.[6]

Creative organizations make an even broader and more effective use of feedback. They understand both the difference between the two forms of feedback and the requirement for both. First, they provide tactical feedback to performers that is accurate, specific, prompt, direct, reliable, and appropriate. Second, they provide feedback from the market at all levels, but particularly at the strategic level. And they *use* the feedback. Chapter 9 describes in more detail how an organization can use both forms of feedback to become and remain a creative learning organization.

What to Do Now

How does your organization stack up as a creative organizational system in terms of the seven basic characteristics? To help you get a clearer picture, here's another simple chart you can use to rate yourself. Each characteristic is listed, followed by the same rating scale used in Chapter 1. For each characteristic, draw an X on the line, rating your organization from 0, if it completely lacks the characteristic, to 10, if it has the characteristic in large measure.

When you finish rating your organization on all seven characteristics, draw a line connecting each of the ratings. Once again, you'll have a snapshot of how your organization looks at present.

The chart isn't designed simply to help you rate your organization. It's followed by specific suggestions that will help you move toward a more creative organization. Pick one or two characteristics to work on and start applying the suggestions.

The Basic Characteristics of a Creative Organizational System

1. My organization understands the relationship between outputs and waste quite differently from the way traditional organizations do.   0———5———10

2. My organization uses waste, surprise, and invisible consequences as a source of opportunity.   0———5———10

3. My organization makes those operating each system responsible for controlling it.   0———5———10

4. My organization provides the individuals who operate systems free access to the resources they need.   0———5———10

5. My organization ensures that each player works both to achieve the overall goals of the organization and to meet specific objectives that support those goals.   0———5———10

6. My organization provides directly to performers tactical feedback that they can use to improve operations.   0———5———10

7. My organization provides and uses feedback from the market at all levels, but particularly at the strategic level.   0———5———10

Evaluate your responses, read the suggestions below, and then select the one or two areas on which you want to work.

1. Does your organization still understand the relationship between outputs and waste in the narrow way that a traditional organization does? No matter how creative you are, you probably have some systems that produce repeatable, clearly defined outputs. You should know exactly what waste each of these systems produces, and those who operate the systems should be reducing it continually. To this extent, you're like a traditional organization. For your creative operations, though, start developing an understanding of which activities help create the product or service and which are waste. For starters, pick a successful project that has just been completed. Review all the activities that went into it and identify those that didn't support its success or even got in the way. Decide how to stop doing those activities. Then stop. But identify waste, here and elsewhere, on the basis of results, not according to an arbitrary definition.

2. *Does your organization not use waste, surprise, and invisible consequences as sources of opportunity?* Think of your organization as pushing its grocery cart, looking in each trash can for something of value. Look at a running system or a completed project and ask yourself these questions:

- Why did we produce this waste? No one intended it. Then why did it happen? Is there an opportunity hidden in it?
- What happened that came as a surprise? Why did it happen? How? What opportunity lies in the unexpected event?
- Are there some invisible consequences hiding around here? Unexplained performer discontent? An unexplained improvement in morale? If a change has occurred, what other operation might have been affected by the change? Have we looked to see?

3. *Does your organization make someone other than those operating each system responsible for controlling it?* You might try this sequence of steps:

- Identify the controls (constraints) placed on the system that are absolutely necessary.
- Start working out plans to transfer these controls to the operators of the system.
- Begin developing the individuals who operate the system so that they can take over more and more of the controls.

- Start creating the appropriate standards and feedback so that the system operators can tell when they are performing successfully.

4. *Does your organization deny the individuals who operate the systems access to the resources they need?* To remedy this, introduce the access along with the steps just listed. Move control over resources in as quickly as the individuals understand the necessary constraints. You can't do this in neat lockstep. Lead at least slightly with access to resources, because this will begin to convince the players concerned that you really are going to change the current situation.

5. *Do the players in your organization do something other than work to achieve the overall goals of the organization and to meet specific objectives that support those goals?* So much has been written on this that there's no need for me to repeat it here. If your players at every level aren't already driven by values, goals, and objectives, start now to see that they are.

6. *Does your organization fail to provide performers with direct tactical feedback that they can use to improve operations?* If it does, don't feel like the Lone Stranger; the best organizations generally succeed only partially at this. Set your goal now to be better than they are. If you have a true TQM process in effect, you're off to a good start. If you don't, start working on the problem today. Call in the staff, but only as advisers and facilitators. Have them go to the players on the floor to find out from those most directly involved the feedback they need. Then give them this feedback. It wouldn't hurt if you did some of this yourself. At the least, make sure that you get briefed regularly on what the staff is finding.

7. *Does your organization not provide and use feedback from the market at all levels, particularly at the strategic level?* Again, if you're really doing TQM, you've at least started on this. Keep going. If you're not getting strategic feedback, start dealing with the problem now. You may find that using an experienced consultant in the beginning stages will save considerable time and effort.

Chapter 3

Why You Must Cultivate Frame Flexibility

God forbid there should be a problem that comes up for which
there isn't a bulletin. That means the problem's *new!*

—Former Sears senior executive, describing
the bureaucratic attitude at Sears

Most power-generating plants run on coal or natural gas; these
fuels are cheap and plentiful, but once you burn them they're
gone for good. Uncreative organizations are a lot like this; they
often burn up, or at least burn out, their best players.

Power-generating plants could use breeder reactors. As they
run, these reactors consume atomic fuel, but they also generate
more fuel than they consume. The more they run, the more fuel
they generate—and this is just how a creative organization operates. Instead of burning out its players, it keeps firing them up
and drawing new ideas from them; it ends with more creativity
than it began with. (The strength of breeder reactors also creates
their greatest problem: what to do with all the radioactive material
they generate. Happily, society doesn't have that problem yet
with surplus creativity.)

In this chapter, we take an extended look at one of the critical
underpinnings of constantly creative organizations: constant
frame flexibility. And at its opposites: being framelocked and
framebound. Once we understand frame flexibility and how

42

critical it is for organizational success and creativity, we'll look at ten attributes of an organization that directly support frame flexibility. Then, as in the previous two chapters, you'll find specific suggestions that you can use to begin developing these attributes in your own organization.

The Power of Frames

Human beings must process immense amounts of information to survive. We accomplish this feat by focusing on certain perceptions and tasks and not others—just as a camera focused on a face will ignore the view from the studio window or the beautiful flowers on the table across the room. And just as the viewfinder of a camera frames the desired picture and cuts out other scenes, when human beings focus on specific problems they frame them in ways that emphasize certain aspects of the situation and ignore others. Here are some familiar examples:

• Parents often devote considerable energy to keeping their teenage children from falling in with "the wrong crowd." Consequently, they frame their teenagers' friends and activities in terms of how they will promote or hinder this basic goal. By doing so, they increase the likelihood that their teens won't fall into bad company. However, they may frame out other possible goals, such as increasing their children's ability to cope with a wide variety of social situations or to experiment with their world.

• A human resources management department may focus on ensuring that the company comply with all EEO, OSHA, and workers' compensation rules. This frame may enable it to deal effectively with problems in these areas. It may also prevent it from focusing effectively on other goals, such as filling jobs rapidly or finding outstanding job candidates.

• A computer company may focus on meeting the hardware and software needs of corporations that use large mainframe computers. This frame may enable it to deliver a high level of service to these customers and perhaps even to become the predominant world player in that market. The frame may also prevent the company from responding to changes in the market that are dramatically reducing the importance of mainframes.

In short, our frames help us focus on certain parts of experience at the cost of ignoring other parts.[1]

How do we build our frames? From a combination of two materials: our goals and our past successes. Let's look at each in turn.

We watch someone taking an action we don't understand and ask: Why is she doing this? Psychoanalysts give one type of answer: She's denying her feelings for her mother. Social learning theorists give another: That's how she was socialized. But the most practical answer, and the one that best explains *this* action in *this* situation, is: She believes it will help achieve one or more of her goals. Whatever else may be true of human beings, our waking hours are dominated by goals: eat breakfast, finish a report, watch the Cowboys' game, and so forth.

To achieve goals, even a simple goal like eating breakfast, we must *focus* our attention and our activities. For short-term goals, we focus on one activity, then another, then another. For longer-term goals, our focus tends to be more constant: If I want a promotion, I may focus constantly on my boss's reaction to me. And this constant, long-term focus is what creates frames.

If my goal is to get promoted, so that I focus on my boss's reactions, that becomes one of the ways I frame my actions. Should I agree to take this project on? Should I complain about the service from reproduction? My basic frame for answering this question is: Will it help get me promoted? How will my boss look at it? My actions will be very different from what they would be if, for instance, my frame were: How can I improve the processes that my job is part of?

We create frames to help us attain goals. We continue to use them over periods of time when we succeed with them; we drop or modify them when they don't produce the right results. If I find that my boss responds favorably when I focus on her reactions, I will use that frame more frequently to guide my actions. Conversely, if she reacts with suspicion or disapproval, I will search for another way to frame my actions. The current frames I use are those that worked for me in the past—which is just another way of saying that I learn from experience. The more successful these frames have been, the more they will seem both "good" and "right" to me.

Individually, we must use frames that maintain our focus so we can achieve our goals; otherwise, our actions will be scattered and ineffective. And it only makes sense to choose the frames that have worked in the past. Organizations follow exactly the same logic. They set strategic goals, focus their efforts on achieving those goals, and develop the frames that will help them to do so.

How Frames Can Go Wrong

For an organization (or individual or group) the greatest strength of frames can also become its greatest weakness. When a company develops a strong focus that succeeds over time, the frames that provide that focus become institutionalized. They become part of the culture of the company. We have ample evidence of how hard it is to change culture.[2] The world may change, even dramatically, but the company continues to see it only through its familiar frames. It has become *framebound.*

An organization becomes framebound when its accustomed frames prevent it from responding effectively to a changing world. In that circumstance, the very frames that have made it successful prevent it from adapting to current conditions. For instance:

- Its sales may be dropping because the market as a whole is shrinking. Instead of dealing with the implications of a shrinking market, it continues to frame the situation as a problem with market share.
- Its changing processes may require greater abilities and formal education even from its lower-paid workers. Instead of understanding the impact of its new work organization it may frame the problem as "Why can't we get productive workers anymore?"
- It is attempting to move into consumer markets but encounters high levels of customer dissatisfaction. Instead of try-

ing to understand its new customers better, it concentrates on its traditional frame of producing technically superior products.

A company may encounter another version of the same problem, this time internally. Individual divisions, departments, and even teams develop their own frames. When these frames become too specialized, too oriented to the work of the subordinate unit itself, individuals in different units can no longer work effectively with one another. Just as traffic may be brought to a standstill by gridlock, an organization may find itself paralyzed by *framelock*. All organizations encounter this problem at some time; for some organizations it can be fatal, as when:

- Marketing cannot understand the problems involved in launching new services and insists on a stream of innovations that is beyond the ability of the company to support.
- Accounting insists that its primary function is to collect data for quarterly and annual reports to stockholders and taxing authorities and refuses to consider implementing a new cost accounting system that would more accurately associate indirect costs with the products that drive them.
- The management information systems department insists on following the full formal development process for a new system, refusing to consider rapid prototyping or other methods that speed up development but require systems analysts to work with customers in new and different ways.

Whether the organization ignores crucial changes in its environment (is framebound) or its parts cannot work effectively with one another (is framelocked), the same condition results: It becomes less competitive—sometimes dramatically so. We've seen the phenomenon again and again in the news: GM and Xerox losing market share in booming markets, Ford and Harley-Davidson almost driven to bankruptcy, IBM's future in question. In the midst of such crises, executives continue to frame circumstances in familiar ways. (Ford, Xerox, and Harley-Davidson managed to reframe their situations in time to avert disaster. The futures of GM and IBM seem less assured.)

Even if a framebound or framelocked company manages to survive, it becomes less and less creative. It overlooks promising alternatives. It deals with problems repetitively, even when its solutions clearly aren't working. As the pressure builds, conformity and orthodoxy become loyalty tests. Everyone circles the wagons and waits for the calvary—which, of course, never arrives.

If you intend to have a constantly creative organization in a constantly changing world you cannot afford a strong culture based on a narrow set of fixed frames. You must instead develop a culture in which all frames are flexible, permitting you to stretch them frequently and creatively. And you must be prepared for a time when you may have to abandon your most cherished frames.

How do you accomplish this daunting task? The next few chapters take up important aspects of the answer. You turn diversity and conflict into an advantage, using them to support multiple perspectives within the company. You use technology in ways that reinforce flexibility, and you develop efficiency by understanding and using the innovation cycle. You hire, develop, promote, and challenge imaginative and flexible people who are willing to experiment with new approaches and ways of framing situations.

None of these actions by themselves, or even in combination, are enough. Your organization must operate from day to day in a way that empowers people's imagination and encourages their flexibility. In the rest of this chapter, we'll look at ten attributes of organizations that support organizational creativity in general and frame flexibility in particular.

I don't pretend that these are all the attributes needed to support frame flexibility; I do believe they're the key ones. You're already familiar with many of them in other contexts, but they're included here because they directly support an organization's ability to be constantly creative. For each attribute, there's an example of its lack, an example of its presence, and a short note on how the attribute supports flexible framing and creativity. At the end of the chapter, you can rate your organization on each of the attributes, and I'll provide suggestions on how your organization can acquire and enhance each attribute.

(A quick note before we begin. After I worked up my preliminary list, I talked with what the news media call "a well-placed source" at Apple Computer. I ran the list by that individual, who made several helpful suggestions. This list, then, describes ten attributes that characterize Apple—which has certainly qualified as a creative *and* successful organization for the past several years.)[3]

Ten Organizational Attributes That Support Flexibility

1. Creative organizations are built on a high level of trust.

What they avoid:

"Ellen, we need your unit to cut its costs at least 5 percent by July."
"Hey, wait a minute—why pick on me?"
"It's not just you. We've got to get our costs in line, and in a hurry."
"Well, why don't you lean on Charlie; he's the one that got all the extra people six months ago. My people are already pushed hard and . . ."

What they do:

"Ellen, we need your unit to cut its costs at least 5 percent by July."
"Wow—that much that soon? It sounds like we're really in a bind."
"We are. We've got to get costs down."
"OK, I'll meet with my people and see what we can do. I'd also like to talk with Charlie and then maybe the three of us could talk. I think we can simplify the processing if you're willing to help us. We might even squeeze out more than 5 percent."
"That's certainly an offer I can't refuse. . . ."

If ideas are the fuel of a creative organization, trust is the lubricant that enables the members, teams, and other units to operate effectively with each other. Without trust, actions must be safe, and nothing is safer than to toe the party line and frame problems in familiar, comfortable ways. Trust provides an environment in which individuals can experiment with different ways of framing situations without jeopardizing their careers.

2. *Creative organizations expect everyone to tell it like it is and also expect everyone to ask the questions necessary to find out how it is.*

What they avoid:

"That about ends what corporate has announced: We're going to have to cut our costs at least 15 percent within the next six months."
"Does that mean some of us may lose our jobs?"
"I'm sorry, Jim, I can't tell you that. I just don't have the information."
"The new system we've been counting on—has it been canceled?"
"I can't tell you anything on that either. . . ."

What they do:

"That's the essence of it: We're going to have to cut our costs at least 15 percent within the next six months."
"Does that mean some of us may lose our jobs?"
"Maybe, but you'll get a voice in that. If corporate can't find the savings in nonlabor expenses in the next two weeks, they're going to let us know. Then they'll listen to us and make a final decision based on everyone's input."
"The new system we've been counting on—has it been canceled?"
"Not yet, but it's one of the options. It depends on. . . ."

What they avoid:

"Max, I hear that Owen & Co. is unhappy with the preliminary report we've given them."

"No big deal, Madeline. We have a couple of small problems, but everything is basically on track. Marie Savage is the one who reviewed it, and you know how picky she is."

"Yeah, I guess you really can't please everybody all the time. . . ."

What they do:

"Max, I hear that Owen & Co. is unhappy with the preliminary report we've given them."

"Yeah, and frankly I'm not sure what it means. Marie Savage reviewed the proposal, and you know how picky she can be. But I'm still uncomfortable."

"Have you looked at the proposal closely?"

"Yeah, and even if my own people did it, I'm still not sure I'm comfortable with it. We're going over it again this afternoon. . . ."

There were two examples for this attribute because telling it like it is a two-way street. Leaders are honest with everyone about the overall situation of the company, and they expect everyone to be honest with them about what's really happening in day-to-day operations. Nothing, I repeat, *nothing* keeps an organization from being framebound and framelocked like a constant diet of honesty.

3. *Creative organizations not only permit but encourage everyone to communicate with everyone else.*

What they avoid:

"Adrena, do I understand that you went and talked directly to Sam Westin in marketing about your project?"

"Yeah, Henry, I did. Don't tell me you're unhappy about that."

"Of course I'm unhappy. How would you feel if the head of the marketing department called you about something you weren't up on? You know you should have gone through channels."

"But I needed an answer, and you weren't here, and I knew that Sam had some experience in the area, and. . . ."

What they do:

"Adrena, do I understand that you went and talked directly to Sam Westin in marketing about your project?"

"Yeah, Henry, I did. We mostly got it settled. He and I are going to go over the only remaining item tomorrow with Ellen Pfister, who's in the Chicago office. I think that will get it settled."

"Good. I was hoping you could take care of this one without my having to get involved. Evidently the new videoconferencing setup is working."

"It sure is. I've talked with Boston, San Antonio—and with Ben Rogers up the street—so far today. . . ."

When trust is high and honesty is expected, no one has anything to fear from unlimited communication. In this way, new ideas move quickly within the organization, stretching frames by their very presence.

Such a free flow of information does create a problem: how to keep the available information from overwhelming everyone. A creative organization gives its members better and better tools with which to separate what's useful to them from what's merely background noise. But it is always the individual members who decide, never someone else who decides for them.

4. When a problem arises, creative organizations look for solutions, not scapegoats; they neither pistol-whip members for making mistakes nor excuse the mistakes.

What they avoid:

"OK, you all know how close we came to losing our shirt on the McClean job because our bid was so low. Now, what do we do about it?"

"Don't look at me, Rafael. Anne and her marketing people pressured us unmercifully to get that bid out; we told them we had no confidence at all in what we came up with."

"If we pressured you, Mitchell, it surely didn't show in your results. I can't for the life of me understand how it can take you so long just to price out a simple project like that one. . . ."

What they do:

"OK, you all know how close we came to losing our shirt on the McClean job because our bid was so low. Now, what do we do about it?"

"No matter how you cut it, Rafael, we were the ones who came up with the lousy figures. We agreed to rush the estimate to help Anne out; I take full responsibility for that. But the next time you need something like that in such a hurry, Anne, I'm just going to have to tell you no."

"I understand your concern, Mitchell, but please don't say no just yet. Anne, do we really need to rush our bids so?"

"Not *rush* them, Rafael. And, Mitchell, I'm sorry if we put too much pressure on you. That wasn't what we intended. But it's murder out there right now, and if we can't respond quickly we're going to lose customers."

"It sounds to me like we need to work on this problem at length. Anne and Mitchell, can the two of you meet with me next Tuesday to see what we can do to help the situation? . . ."

Blaming, an everyday activity in many organizations, pulverizes creativity in short order. The more blame there is, the more organizations retreat into their safe and comfortable frames. Conversely, when no one is being blamed, everyone has the chance to expand his or her frames and explore new options.

Remember, creative organizations care even more about performance than traditional organizations do. No one gets off the hook. But simply because a traditional organization is so often into blaming, performance seldom improves. A creative organization's approach is completely different—and it works far better. It relies heavily on goals, commitment, and constant feedback.

5. Creative organizations focus on problems and opportunities, not on personalities and power structures.

What they avoid:

"Betti, what do you think we ought to do for an improvement project this month?"

"Vince, I neither know nor care. Bob Lynch will get on his soapbox about costs, and we'll do another cost project."

"But you know that's not where the problem is."

"Of course I know, but why fight City Hall? You want to be the one that crosses Lynch? . . ."

What they do:

"Betti, what do you think we ought to do for an improvement project this month?"

"Vince, I'm sick of these cost-containment drives we've been having. I think we need to work the quality side for a while."

"You're probably right, but you know Bob Lynch is going to push for another cost project."

"Let him. I'll listen to him, and maybe he's right. But I've been talking to some key customers, and I think what they have to say will get everyone's attention. Even when I lost out last month, everybody did listen. . . ."

Creative organizations know that opportunity lies only in the present and the future—never in the past. They sift the past for lessons to be learned, but then move on to the present to apply those lessons. And they know they can't afford the luxury of making key decisions on "political" grounds. Again, they're free to explore new frames and new options.

6. Creative organizations use shared values, goals, and objectives to support and enhance self-management.

I'm not going to bother to illustrate this; self-management is key to every form of empowerment, every self-managed team, every approach capable of responding quickly to changes in the environment. And self-management is key to frame flexibility, because an organization's current frames change most easily in the interchange between self-confident and empowered individuals.

7. Creative organizations include their customers and suppliers in their decision-making processes.

This is another one I'm not going to illustrate. If you don't know by now that effective companies of all kinds treat their customers and suppliers as an intrinsic part of their operations, you've probably been wrestling alligators in the Louisiana swamps for the last decade. In case you have, you should know that, according to James Bryan Quinn, some two-thirds of innovations in the industries that have been studied come from the customer-supplier interface.[4] Creative organizations, however, have an even greater incentive to do this. What better source of new ideas to change and expand frames effectively is there than a constant dialogue with customers and suppliers?

8. Creative organizations are always scanning the horizon and proactively anticipating change: they are skilled at creating their future.

What they avoid:

"Paul, it's murder out there. We just lost the Reed & Thompson account, we're burning overtime like there's no tomorrow and still falling behind, and I've heard rumors that Dennis is just going to call it quits and retire."
"I know. When will the pressure ever let up?"
"With all we're doing, you'd think something would be working. Well, maybe next month things will be a little more normal. . . ."

What they do:

"Paul, if this business gets much more exciting I don't think I can stand it. Jayne's brainstorm last week floored the Reed &

Thompson people; we may have to bring another half-dozen people on board to service that one account."

"Tell me about it. I had almost a daylong meeting with my folks and we've worked out an approach that ought to cut overtime at least in half within a month without cutting our output. By the way, have you seen Dennis lately?"

"Lord, no. He's been so busy running around the country 'taking the temperature of the market' that no one sees him. But we sure do get an endless stream of 'look into this' and 'have you considered that?' notes by E-mail. . . ."

Remember, Peter Senge believes that a true learning organization is "continually expanding its capacity to create its future." At its core, this means that the organization consciously examines and adjusts its existing frames, and sometimes even moves to very different ones, to stay abreast of changes in the world around it.

9. Creative organizations promote ownership and entrepreneurship everywhere.

What they avoid:

"Elaine, your idea about trying to sell our project management courses to some of our customers was great. I've asked Tom Whiting to pick your brain and get the venture under way as quick as he can."

"Roger, do you mean Tom is going to run it? After all, it was my idea."

"Now, now, Elaine, don't get defensive. You know that Tom has much more experience than you do. Besides, you can count on a nice, big bonus for the idea. . . ."

What they do:

"Elaine, your idea of trying to sell our project management courses to some of our customers was great. It's your idea, so you ought to be the one to do it, but do you think you have enough experience to head it up?"

"By myself, maybe not. But I talked to Tom Whiting and

we've agreed to work together on the development. Both of us want to do it, and we'll work out a joint recommendation by August 1 and present it to you."

"How come we're just sitting here? Go after it!"

Nothing builds commitment like a piece of the action. If you want ideas from individuals, see that their ideas pay off directly for them—but not through a corporate suggestion program. Let them use their ideas to enlarge their jobs, move the company in a new direction, even create a start-up. The ownership doesn't have to be figurative. A Rutgers University study conducted in 1991 and 1992 showed that companies with high employee ownership consistently outperformed those without it.[5]

Want to really stretch frames and insure yourself against being framebound? Just hold out the prospect to every individual that a bright idea can lead to new responsibility and opportunity—and higher income! Studies show conclusively that new ideas require persistent, committed champions if they are to succeed; and nothing encourages champions like the knowledge that they can take responsibility for what they propose and sink or swim with it. (Of course, the larger organization retains responsibility for ensuring that the odds favor swimming.)

Here's a final interesting thought about developing entrepreneurship. Donald Hicks studied what happened to jobs in the Dallas area from 1986 through early 1989. He found that overall employment changed little over these three years. However, 27 percent of the jobs that existed at the beginning of 1986 had vanished by 1989. Most of these jobs were replaced by new ones, and *61 percent* of the new jobs were created by entrepreneurs starting new businesses. If this is typical of business in general, and it probably is, just think what might have happened if some of these new businesses had been spawned by entrepreneurs from *within* existing businesses. A lot more businesses might have survived, and those that survived might have been a lot more prosperous. Think about it.[6]

10. Creative organizations encourage play, daydreaming, and even silliness.

I won't try to illustrate this one, either; after all, you'd probably think it was silly!

You may find this a hard pill to swallow, but sustained creativity requires this freedom from the everyday demands of work. An individual or organization simply cannot be sober and goal-directed all of the time and still maintain its creative edge. Creativity requires spontaneity, and spontaneity emerges as play. Watch any creative team. You may see it absorbed in its task, then suddenly explode in a flurry of awful jokes or unrestrained silliness. Or you may see someone "tune out" the group to daydream about how a particular line of thought might work out.

Creativity exhilarates, but sustained creativity also drains energy. Play, daydreaming, and silliness not only support creativity but provide relief from the demanding work of creating. They do more; in the movement from serious concentration to play, we increase our ability to jump over existing frames, look at them from new and weird angles, stretch and pull them into novel forms. Unconstrained spontaneity provides the final and best line of defense against becoming framebound and framelocked.

What to Do Now

It's time to stop talking and start looking—specifically, to start looking at how your organization stacks up on the ten attributes of a flexible organization. As with Chapters 1 and 2, this chapter ends with a list of the attributes, followed by the same simple rating scale. For each attribute, rate your organization from 0 (not true of it at all) to 10 (completely true of it). Then connect the individual ratings, look at the overall picture they present, read the suggestions for developing each attribute, and choose one or two to begin working on immediately. Once again, you won't create a constantly creative organization overnight, but you will begin to move in the right direction. And each step makes the subsequent steps easier.

The Ten Attributes of a Flexible Organization

1. Our organization is built on a high level of
   trust.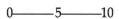

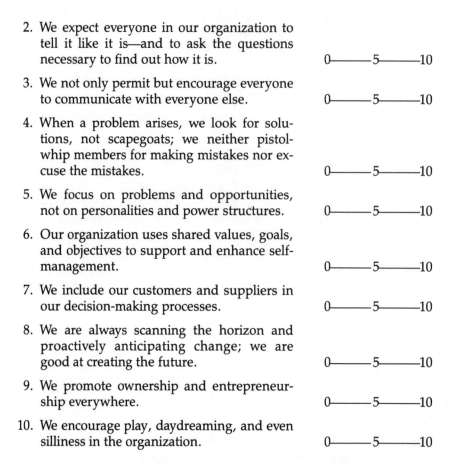

2. We expect everyone in our organization to tell it like it is—and to ask the questions necessary to find out how it is.　　0———5———10

3. We not only permit but encourage everyone to communicate with everyone else.　　0———5———10

4. When a problem arises, we look for solutions, not scapegoats; we neither pistol-whip members for making mistakes nor excuse the mistakes.　　0———5———10

5. We focus on problems and opportunities, not on personalities and power structures.　　0———5———10

6. Our organization uses shared values, goals, and objectives to support and enhance self-management.　　0———5———10

7. We include our customers and suppliers in our decision-making processes.　　0———5———10

8. We are always scanning the horizon and proactively anticipating change; we are good at creating the future.　　0———5———10

9. We promote ownership and entrepreneurship everywhere.　　0———5———10

10. We encourage play, daydreaming, and even silliness in the organization.　　0———5———10

Once again, you've created a quick visual profile of your organization as it is today; now you can choose where to begin changing it. For each of the ten qualities listed there is a corresponding suggestion below. After you've thought about the qualities and read the ten suggestions, choose one or two suggestions to implement beginning tomorrow morning.

1. *Does your organization lack a high level of trust?* You have no chance at all of building any form of high-performance organization if you do not build it on trust. You can implement one key component of trust immediately. Make this policy, and then enforce it: Everyone is to consider carefully before making commitments and then is to keep every commitment *to the letter,*

every time. If conditions change and they can't? Renegotiate the commitment immediately. (Anyone walking in on the last day and announcing that he or she can't keep a commitment will be required to distribute cards saying "I am a wimp" outside the local supermarket for an hour on Saturday.) Make this an unbending policy and institutionalize it. You may be amazed at how much this one policy will do for your operations.

2. *Do members of your organization try to avoid telling it like it is, and do you discourage them from asking the questions necessary to find out how it is?* If this is the situation, you have a long, hard row to hoe. Make sure you develop trust throughout the organization; that comes first. Then use the trust to bring honesty in. Set the pace yourself. Start sharing the news, good and bad. Pick your audience carefully at first, but start being up-front when you make a mistake. Perhaps you might begin by publicly apologizing to someone you overruled but who turned out to be right.

As part of opening up the organization, establish a simple three-part policy: (1) Everyone is free to speak his or her mind. (2) Everyone is expected to treat everyone else and everyone else's opinion with complete respect. (3) Everyone has the right to be heard, but no one is guaranteed that his or her point of view will prevail. Besides helping to promote honesty, this policy will help support every one of the ten qualities—and particularly the next three.

3. *Do you fail to encourage everyone to communicate with everyone else?* Get proficient at the first two attributes, and internal communications will begin to fall into line. Thank people when they communicate sideways or diagonally and get a problem resolved. (In fact, thank anyone who solves a problem without involving you.) Think you're communicating well now? Double or triple the amount you communicate. Keep pushing, keep rewarding people for talking to other people. If you don't have E-mail, perhaps you should consider installing it.

4. *When a problem arises, do you look for scapegoats; do you blame members for making mistakes and not let them learn from their mistakes?* The remedy here is simple: STOP! Announce clearly and forcefully that you are changing the way you do business. Set the example; don't look for or accept any scapegoats yourself. Don't

let your people do it either. (Here's a simple policy you can enforce. Don't let anyone complain about anyone else unless that person is present. If someone has a complaint, insist that he or she come to see you with whoever is causing the problem. Then let the individual make the complaint face-to-face. If necessary, be the moderator. You'll want to accompany this by building trust and insisting on effective performance and learning; if not, players will be tempted simply to hide the problems.

5. *Do you focus on personalities and power structures rather than on problems and opportunities?* As with #2, this habit may have burrowed deeply within your organizational culture. You won't dig it out overnight. Work on the first three items in the list; each success will diminish this habit a little. Try gently but forcefully to keep discussions focused on the issues; just as forcefully, prevent any attempts at power plays. You'll succeed; it just takes patience.

6. *Does your organization not use shared values, goals, and objectives to support and develop self-management?* The shelves of libraries and bookstores everywhere sag with books on self-management and empowerment. (Every one of my previous five books dealt with the topic in some way.) Colleges and commercial training firms will teach you how to empower your organization, as will legions of consultants. I suggest that you find a manager with an operation like your own who has already moved toward an empowering organization and learn all you can. Take your time on this one, but be persistent. We know that the most productive individuals are those who have clear and worthwhile goals *and* the autonomy to pursue them in their own way. But it all depends on self-management; develop it as you empower your organization.

7. *Do you exclude your customers and suppliers from your decision-making processes?* On one level, you can change this easily: Just do it. However, your organization may believe that it has nothing to learn from customers and that the best way to deal with suppliers is to keep them at arm's length and let them compete with one another. That makes including them in your decision making a major cultural change. You might want to begin by targeting a specific customer or group of customers who

are particularly progressive and using them in a planning session. Or by holding a face-to-face meeting with a particularly dependable supplier to explore how you might strengthen your relationship to your mutual advantage.

Are your customers and suppliers internal? Nothing really changes when that's the case except that meeting with them should be even easier. Set up regular meetings with your customers, individually or en masse. If that helps, survey them to find out how well you're meeting their needs. Develop the kind of relationship in which you can regularly solicit their ideas for improving your service to them. Hold the same meetings with your suppliers; one effective place to begin is by asking "How can we be a better customer?" Then go on from there.

8. *Do you not scan the horizon and proactively anticipate change; are you not skilled at creating your future?* Many organizations fail to stay one step ahead of the future because they are too preoccupied with their current operating problems—how to control costs, how to meet schedules, how to keep up with competitors. This absorption in the present becomes a way of life; no one has time for anything unless it has immediate productive results. An organization escapes from this situation in only one way: The senior leaders decide to reallocate how time is spent. Normally, you can do this most effectively by giving a small group of individuals the responsibility rather than by spreading it widely. Then insist that the group meet regularly with you to share the results of their work. And don't ever postpone meetings because *you're* too busy working on current problems.

9. *Do you fail to promote ownership and entrepreneurship everywhere?* You may not be in good company here, but you certainly have a lot of company. Many organizations talk about "ownership," but all too few of them truly use its power. There's no quick and easy way to change this situation. As you empower players at all levels, their feelings of ownership will grow. Then, when someone gets a really good idea, give that person as much responsibility as possible for implementing the idea. This will begin to spread authority more widely within the organization; that's why you need to combine it with the general move toward empowerment and self-management. Just keep working patiently

toward a situation in which the organization is really a "holding company" for entrepreneurs and teams of entrepreneurs.

10. *Do you discourage play, daydreaming, and silliness in your organization?* If the organization has no room for play and silliness now, introducing spontaneity will certainly challenge you, particularly in that most people will see it as just "goofing off." I know of no easy solutions. If you've been frowning on individuals or groups that seemed to be having too much fun, you can stop. When someone contributes a joke or silly comment that breaks the tension or directs everyone's attention to more productive channels, recognize the wisdom in the wit. You might want to have an experienced "humor consultant" work with your senior leadership group. Be careful with this one, though. A good consultant may help the process, but the impetus for change has to come from the organization itself.

Chapter 4

How to Use Diversity and Conflict Creatively

> The fastest way to learn is to discover a person or group which reaches totally different conclusions to your own when looking at the same reality.
>
> —Robert Theobald

As I begin this chapter, *diversity* is the watchword of the hour. If I pick up a magazine the odds are excellent that some article will deal with "diversity." New books promoting diversity appear monthly, perhaps even more often. But just what is this diversity we talk about, and what does it have to do with the constantly creative organization?

Superficially, diversity results from major changes in the makeup of the American work force that took place in the 1980s and continue into the 1990s. The United States has large African-American, Hispanic, Asian-American, and Native American populations, and these make up a larger and larger percentage of the total work force. Individuals are immigrating to the United States from countries all over the world; the two coasts feel the heaviest impact, but no city in the nation escapes this impact. Women have moved into and upward in organizations in record numbers. And Americans are developing new attitudes toward the disabled, homosexuals, and others who were formerly barred from the mainstream.

But is this diversity? Yes—and no. For a creative organization, diversity can contribute energy and imagination. It can also be a rich source of multiple perspectives. But it matters just how the organization understands diversity and how it responds to it. That's what this chapter is about.

Just What Is Diversity?

To begin, we need to understand what diversity means from the organization's point of view. It did *not* come into being in the eighties or nineties. It is not simply a product of the growth of African-American, Asian-American, Hispanic-American, and other hyphenated American movements of the last decade. Just the reverse; the current "diversity" movement is yet another ingredient in the overall diversity of American organizations.

Organizational diversity begins with the occupational and functional diversity that occurs in every organization. Accountants see the organization very differently from the way marketers do. Engineers see it differently from the way human resource specialists do. Managers see it differently from the way workers see it. Top-level managers see it from a perspective different from that of first-level managers. And so on, through every different occupational and functional group, through all the horizontal and vertical divisions of the organization. The average organization has always had more diversity than it could deal with, which is why Chapter 3 centered on framelock, one product of this diversity.

To this, we now add another version of diversity, based on ethnic, sexual, and other differences. When we read about diversity in newspapers and magazines, this is the diversity being discussed. Of course, even this isn't always clear.

Some writers apparently see diversity as an extension of the EEO efforts of the past three decades. Here, diversity means that organizations employ, in a range of occupations and at a range of levels, members of recognized minority groups and females. Thus, an organization is "diverse" if it has the proper representation of African-Americans, Hispanics, Asian-Americans, women, and other identified minorities or protected categories.

Others treat diversity as different cultural traits that need to be understood, usually through some form of "diversity training." Much of this training is designed to help members of various groups—but particularly white males—to understand the basic differences among these groups. In this training, individuals—again, largely white males—in one cultural group can learn to understand the meaning of the behavior of members of other groups and thus enhance communication across cultural lines.

There are, of course, many other variations. The most prevalent of these variations is the definition of diversity as *cultural diversity.* For its proponents, diversity includes appreciation of different ethnic groups as well as of females, the disabled, homosexuals, and other groups previously excluded from mainstream American life. Many prominent spokespersons for this understanding present diversity as a positive good in itself, generally with a moral cast to their pronouncements. In its extreme form, valuing diversity in this way means striking back at "Eurocentric" culture and practicing campus "political correctness."

Because this version of diversity is so prevalent today, let me make a few comments on it before we move on. I believe that this understanding of diversity has two significant strengths and two major weaknesses, and both of these need to be understood.

1. Its first strength is that it points directly to the very real differences among the *values* of different groups. Women often do look at situations differently than men. Hispanic-Americans often have a perspective different from that of Asian-Americans or African-Americans or "mainstream" Americans. These differences *matter*; they reflect significant underlying contrasts in the way individuals in various groups approach life.

2. Its second strength is its understanding that diversity contains significant potential for conflict. Remember the forceful complaint several years ago by Asian-Americans that they were being denied the admission to top universities that their academic achievements merited? Or the current firefight over "political correctness"? In many ways, these are merely the tip of the proverbial iceberg.

An organization must accept and deal openly with both the differences *and* the potential for conflict if it is to use diversity as a source of multiple perspectives and thus of creativity. However, because of the two weaknesses of this understanding of diversity, no organization can settle for the idea that diversity is simply intercultural and intersexual difference.

1. The two weaknesses are interrelated, and each is a variation on a very old theme. I grew up a white male in the American South, and I was halfway through college before the U.S. Supreme Court decided *Brown* v. *Board of Education*. All during my youth, people told me that all "colored people" had certain attributes—many but not all of them unflattering. Today, when I listen to other people tell me that Asian-Americans are this way and African-Americans are that way, I hear the same stereotyping. Now we use "good" or "neutral" stereotypes, but they are stereotypes nonetheless. The first weakness, then, is that as long as we treat cultural differences as somehow absolute, we will continue to speak in stereotypes.

2. The second weakness is this: A focus on cultural and group differences tends to "balkanize" groups, including groups in organizations. That is, diversity becomes divisive: different groups pull away from one another, and life together becomes a bitter struggle to ensure that no other group gets preference over one's own.

The 1992 Los Angeles rioting illustrated this vividly. The initial rioters made a simple black-white distinction; "black" was good; "white" was bad. Never mind that the beaten "whites" consisted mostly of poor Hispanics, poor Asians, and Anglo blue-collar workers. (One individual who narrowly escaped, with a demolished windshield, had been a community activist for years.) Brutality in any form is bad enough; it does not need the additional fuel of race or culture.

A creative organization needs to profit from diversity, but it cannot profit from stereotyping and balkanization. This leads to a final and more inclusive understanding of diversity.

Diversity as a Multifaceted Human Phenomenon

A recent book by John E. Schwarz and Thomas J. Volgy captures succinctly what the purely group (cultural, ethnic, sexual) understanding of diversity omits:

Unlike many peoples, Americans do not have a common blood, religion, race, or language. Absent the bonds that often link individuals in a nation, Americans have forged a national identify and sense of connection to one another out of other materials. They have done so, to a considerable extent, through a shared philosophy founded upon a belief in the promise, possibilities, and progress of the individual.

At its core, the [American] ethos is a belief in inclusion. It is a belief that all can belong no matter what their background or station, that everyone can succeed.[1]

In other words, when proponents of diversity concentrate solely on a group and cultural differences, they ignore the driving force behind the American acceptance of diversity: belief in the power of the individual. Cultural differences are important, but focusing on them to the exclusion of individual differences overlooks the dynamic that has led to the success of repeated waves of immigrants in this country. (It also overlooks the fact that most cultural stereotypes are confining if not suffocating. If you doubt this, ask a Japanese teenage girl who just spent three years in suburban Columbus, Ohio, how she feels about returning to Japan. Or ask an African-American boy in an inner-city ghetto who gets made fun of every day by his peers because he wants to make good grades and go to college how he feels.)

We have finally come to the only understanding of diversity that can genuinely empower creative organizations. Diversity is a product of cultural, group, sexual, functional, and occupational differences. It is just as surely a product of *individual* differences. In fact, it is only the acceptance of the validity of individual differences that can temper the divisive effects of a purely multicultural (and thus ultimately rigid) understanding of diversity.

How a Creative Organization Profits From Diversity

An organization becomes and remains creative when it has the ability to flexibly frame the problems it encounters. When the organization values and uses the multiple perspectives contained within it, it strengthens its frame flexibility. The more diversity the organization can manage, the greater is its potential for multiple perspectives and, with it, the potential for frame flexibility and continuing creativity.

This is a lofty goal, and it takes a mighty effort to reach it. An organization must work constantly to achieve it. What can you and your organization do? Here are a few suggestions.

You can ensure that everyone focuses on the organization's goals. We've already seen that a constantly creative organization must focus on goals to succeed. Once diversity enters the picture, this goal focus becomes even more important—in two different but related ways:

1. When an organization focuses on clear goals that are widely understood, it opens the way for different individuals to achieve these goals in different ways. One reason traditional organizations have great difficulty profiting from diversity is that they are so often committed to the "one right way." Only certain departments, such as industrial engineering, have the authority to change this way. Obviously, such an organization will not welcome functional, cultural, or individual diversity.

On the other hand, focusing on goals rather than on the means to achieve them increases an organization's flexibility and its consequent capacity to use diversity. The organization can entertain the idea that diversity is best dealt with as a dynamic phenomenon, not as a static one. In this environment, diversity and flexibility become mutually supporting; each strengthens the other.[2]

2. The converse of this is equally important: Diversity can exist *only* when everyone is committed to the organization's goals. The organization's goals must take precedence over any and all goals of individuals and groups, whether these are based on occupation and function, on sex, culture, or group, or on individual ambition and desires. This simply is nonnegotiable.

An organization does not exist primarily to allow groups and individuals to achieve their aims; it exists to make an economic, social, and/or political contribution to society. If an organization is to fulfill this function, all its members must be committed to the overall goals and to the specific objectives relevant to their jobs. It is particularly important that individuals committed to achieving "diversity" goals of every kind understand and support this.

You can ensure that the organization accepts and furthers individual and group goals. An organization that concentrates on its overall goals to the exclusion of the goals of its members will never be creative and probably won't even survive for long. Individuals (whether acting as individuals or as members of groups) only commit their energies to broader goals that will help them achieve their own goals. An organization will succeed only when its members believe that the organization's success will also make them successful.

Every successful manager knows that even in the best of circumstances balancing the goals of the organization with the goals of the individuals who compose it is often a variation of one-armed paperhanging. Ambitious individuals and functions compete with one another for power and status—and sometimes even to capture the organization for themselves. Add a multicultural work force to this mix and the potential for explosion rises that much more. Just as exploding gasoline drives a car, however, the energy contained in this diversity can propel an organization to continual creativity. It must be accepted, not denied—but only in the context of the organization's mission, its strategic goals, and the objectives based on them.

You can develop an organization that not only permits but encourages everyone to communicate with everyone else. You read this in Chapter 3; it's one of the basic attributes of a constantly creative organization. All ten of the attributes are critical; by promoting flexibility they help an organization deal with diversity and draw strength from it. In this context, however, constant communication stands out as the indispensable attribute. The organization must insist that members of different groups talk continually with one another, and especially that members of minority groups talk with members of the majority culture. When companies use multifunctional teams, they lead specialists and specialist groups to overcome their narrow frames of reference. The same approach should be taken when dealing with different cultural, ethnic, sexual, and other groups: They must be encouraged, and if necessary pushed, to communicate with one another.

I just can't stress this too much. The tendency of every individual or group that feels excluded is to withdraw, just as the tendency of those who exclude them is to withdraw from them. *You must not let this happen.* If it does, you will spend countless hours, months, or years from now attempting to tear down the barriers that they have erected against one another.

As you ensure that they communicate, I'd suggest that you avoid any spokesperson for any group who has not been chosen (and can be unchosen) by that group. We're so accustomed to self-selected spokespersons that it seems the most natural thing in the world. It isn't. People really are individuals, and anyone who claims to be a spokesperson will inevitably be promoting his own agenda. Only if the group he claims to represent has some control over the person does he have a reason to find out what they want and to present it.

This holds just as true for anyone designated by the organization. We are accustomed to EEO officers and similar positions in the organization; I am not advocating that you abolish them if you have them. But the role of an organizational EEO official is *not* to act as a representative for cultural or other groups. Ideally, she will help individuals in these groups to speak for themselves and their groups. She must also push to see that they are heard by the organization at large; that relative justice is done each individual and group; and that channels for their complaints are open and the complaints responded to. And that is where her responsibilities should end.

Why reject self-appointed or organizationally appointed spokespersons? After all, this setup can be quite convenient. Yes it can—and quite counterproductive too. Whatever the external problem that members of minority cultures face, many of them face an even more serious internal problem: They do not believe in their own power as individuals. When this happens, someone always shows up to take advantage of the situation and to act in their stead. This only reinforces their feelings of personal powerlessness. A constantly creative organization depends on all its members being powerful. You want them to learn that they can resolve their own problems.

I have no general solution for how to do this. I can tell you this much: If your organization is based on teams or other forms of small groups, you have a most effective means right at hand. Your teams should reflect the diversity of the organization and never be composed of just one cultural group. And each team should have the responsibility to integrate everyone into it as a core responsibility. If teams understand this, and particularly if they're aided by sensitive facilitators, you will build the strengths of diversity into the very heart of the organization—precisely where it belongs.

If you don't yet make widespread use of teams, at least apply the basic principle as widely as you can: Keep everyone in contact with individuals from other groups and do it in the smallest, most cohesive setting possible. Above all, do not let cultural or ethnic lines coincide with functional lines. You don't need ethnic competition added to the significant distance engineers and salespersons already feel from one another.

Perhaps it's time for a quick reminder that this chapter isn't really about diversity, its benefits and problems. We're not trying to solve the puzzle of diversity. We are trying to create and maintain the multiple perspectives that keep an organization from becoming framelocked and framebound. Properly managed, work force diversity helps us to do this. No matter how well we manage diversity, however, it will always involve conflict; managing diversity *means* dealing creatively with conflict. It's time to look at just what that means.

How to Use Conflict Creatively

It is basically this simple: If an organization accepts the value of diversity *it also accepts the inevitability of conflict.* A creative organization surfaces and faces conflict, and it resolves it whenever it can, but it never banishes it.

A general manager in a major American corporation puts it this way:

You must keep the conflicts alive and on the surface. Once you have identified the conflicts you see to it that *they* [the managers with the conflicts] resolve them and that they let you know the results. If they agree ahead of time, too quickly, that can shield you from legitimate conflict. *It breaks your heart when you see people have stopped talking about it.*[3]

He based his comments on a simple fact: The operation of any organization generates conflict. Different individuals and groups have different goals that may be mutually contradictory. This conflict may include different ethnic groups vying for power and status in an organization, but it also includes such traditional conflict as that between accounting and human resources, or between partners over the direction a firm should take. It always includes different individuals competing with one another—for promotion, for influence, for power—whether they are members of different cultural groups or not. Conflicts such as these will never vanish from any organization.

All conflict arises from the same basic source: the conflicting goals of individuals, groups, and organizations. Note that it springs from *conflicting* goals, not simply from *different* goals. Conflict arises when individuals become angry, and often frightened, because they believe their own goals are threatened by the goals of others. Politicians run constantly on the theme that "we" aren't getting our fair share and "they" are getting too much. (The whole conflagration in what used to be Yugoslavia was lit with precisely this appeal to Serbs.)

In most companies, this conflict surfaces only partially, if at all. Much of it remains beneath the surface, poisoning relationships and reducing performance throughout the organization. When forced underground, it often engenders another form of conflict, one that arises when the needs, goals, and ideas of individuals and groups are systematically ignored by the organization. Then the original conflict becomes overlaid with alienation and resentment.

Organizations have often generated conflict in this form; excluded individuals have been labeled as "troublemakers," or "old fogies," or otherwise discounted. Entire functions have been treated as organizational stepchildren ("Do we really have to put up with those people in human resources?"). Add to this the groups (blacks, females, gays, the disabled) that have been systematically ignored and discounted, and the level of resentment and alienation creates a barrier that no enlightened diversity policy or diversity training by itself can remove.

Consider this almost trivial example of just how strong the power of alienation is. In the mid-1960s, I worked for a year and a half in Utah. During this period I lived in a small town in which non-Mormons had lived for less than a decade. The town was still very much a Mormon town, with non-Mormons very much in the minority. When we "gentiles" held our Lenten interdenominational study group, guess what?—we spent almost the entire time complaining about the Mormons and their treatment of non-Mormons.

Note that I am not alleging that non-Mormons were badly treated by Mormons; on the whole, I do not believe we were. But what I did experience was a group of people from the country's dominant culture who in a matter of weeks or months had come to feel excluded and as a result developed a palpable resentment of the subculture in which they found themselves. If this can be produced by the experience of a few months, how much deeper do the pain and resentment caused by years of exclusion run?

Here is the point: An organization that intends to manage and profit from diversity must be prepared to bring to the surface and then resolve both the conflict that springs from different goals and the conflict that arises from exclusion. How does it accomplish this? This chapter has already covered three keys:

1. It manages by goals instead of rules, and it keeps everyone focused on the goals. Remember, the basic source of conflict is conflicting goals. If everyone is genuinely committed to organizational goals, this becomes a source of strength to build on.
2. It integrates everyone, whether part of a recognized minority group or not, as fully as possible into the organization. Where the organization is based on teams, integration takes place at that level. It never permits a group to isolate itself and to break off dialogue with others.

3. It permits and encourages each individual to speak for himself or herself; it does not allow either self-appointed or organizationally appointed spokespersons to usurp the individual's prerogative.

In other words, the same qualities that permit an organization to profit from diversity help it to deal effectively with conflict. This is hardly surprising; when an organization demonstrates that it values the needs, goals, and ideas of everyone, resentment and alienation can be replaced by effective advocacy.

Part and parcel of this, however, must be the establishment of effective conflict-reduction and conflict-management methods. We already know how important it is for teams to become proficient at conflict management; if they do not, they will fall victim to a fatal "groupthink." An organization that intends to become continually creative must be just as proficient at managing conflict—and at every level.

This is the good news: New books, seminars, and consultants dealing with conflict resolution appear on the scene every day. This is the bad news: Many of them simply rehash the methods of others. Any selection is bound to be biased, but I have found these books to be useful:

- Roger Fisher and William Ury wrote *Getting to Yes* in 1981; it has since become a classic on how to resolve conflict by identifying common goals.
- Another author who takes a similar approach is Dudley Weeks, whose *The Eight Essential Steps to Conflict Resolution* appeared in 1992. His book and Fisher and Ury's are particularly useful when both parties to the conflict share a desire to resolve it.
- Ury went on to write *Getting Past No: Negotiating with Difficult People* in 1991. In this, he sets forth methods of negotiation that work even when one of the parties seems to have no interest in resolving the conflict. An organization that has high levels of conflict may find this approach the most useful one.
- Arnold Mindell's *The Leader as Martial Artist* (1992) is one of the most creative works ever written on conflict. His meth-

ods are not for the faint of heart, however. They are most apt to succeed either in organizations characterized by dramatic internal conflict or in those that are expert at resolving ordinary levels of conflict and want to push their expertise even further.

Before we leave the topic of conflict management, one last point begs to be made. Any organization should be characterized by mutual respect, but this is especially true of a creative organization. When ideas are springing up and are being debated constantly, attacking the individuals who spring the ideas is simply suicidal. I would go so far as to say that an individual earns the right to be heard only by completely respecting this right in others.

Dealing with issues of diversity requires this same mutual respect. However, when diversity becomes conflict—and it doesn't matter whether the diversity is individual, cultural, sexual, or organizational—too narrow an understanding of mutual respect can get in the way. When deep issues are on the table, deep emotions accompany them. There may be times when a no-holds-barred screaming match provides the only vehicle for gut issues to get heard.

Any organization that intends to resolve serious conflict within its ranks must be prepared for this. It must have individuals competent to decide when it is appropriate to let go and get down and dirty—and then competent to go through the process with the participants. But the organization and the individuals must also have the competence to put the situation back together again, to help bind up the wounds, and, most important, to help find the way out of the conflict.

When Not to Deal With Diversity and Conflict

As I have emphasized throughout this chapter, the creative organization uses both diversity and conflict to its advantage, particularly as a means of fostering multiple perspectives on its problems. But diversity and conflict aren't ends in themselves. How do you tell if your organization is spending too much time working on them, to the detriment of its overall performance? As you might expect, there are no hard-and-fast answers. But these three points, which build on ideas developed earlier in the chapter, can help you make decisions appropriate to your own situation:

1. When dealing with diversity and conflict becomes an end in itself, taking precedence over the organization's primary goals, things have gotten out of hand. Dealing with diversity and conflict can be interesting and stimulating, so much so that individuals may prefer it to the daily business of meeting organizational objectives. No matter how fruitful the process may seem, when this happens the time has come to wind it back down for a while.

2. But suppose someone (or some group) says: "That's just an excuse to stop dealing with us!" Actually, there's a relatively simple test. Has the individual or group had a chance to present its points and be heard? When an organization deals with conflict, there often comes a time when the parties involved just keep bringing up the same old points. When that happens, the situation is stuck, and it's time to jump out of the quagmire. However, this works only when everyone has had the opportunity to present their point of view.

And if an individual or group still claims that it's being ignored, what then? One alternative, if this occurs frequently, is to find a point that can be tested quickly and easily, even if the majority doesn't agree with it. Suppose a number of women feel that the rating system used for salary increases is weighted toward men. Can a small change be made in the plan that will test their belief? Try the change, evaluate it, then decide on the appropriate next action.

3. The final point is this: The organization should provide everyone with the opportunity to be heard, but with no commitment that any specific point will be accepted. We all want the opportunity to be heard, and most of us, if we believe we have been heard, will accept a course of action different from the one we preferred. Everyone should be guaranteed an honest and open hearing. No one should be guaranteed what he or she or the group wants.

Why? Because the goal of diversity and conflict management is *inquiry*, not *advocacy*. People in conflict often begin by advocating a particular position. "The way to deal with this situation is to get costs down, now!" Others state their position in opposition, and the conflict is on. This never resolves conflict. Positions may be put on the table by advocates and may have advocates throughout the discussion. But unless the parties are committed to working through their initial positions to find the best possible solution for the problem, conflict will never be resolved. Win or lose, "your" position or "mine" must ultimately give way to "this is the solution that will work."

What to Do Now

Now it's time to rate your organization on eight factors directly related to its ability to use diversity and conflict to promote creativity. Just mark each item as you did the ones in previous chapters, then connect your marks to create a simple graph of your current situation.

Using Diversity and Conflict

1. Our organization has taken positive steps to ensure that all positions, including those at the very highest levels in our organization, are open to *everyone*.   0———5———10

2. We understand and actively further diversity without limiting it to a narrow multicultural understanding.   0———5———10

3. In policy and in fact, we communicate to all our members at all levels that they are important players, essential to the success of the organization.   0———5———10

4. We ensure that everyone focuses on goals and the objectives required to achieve them, not on narrow requirements or procedures.   0———5———10

5. We accept the validity of the individual goals and needs of *all* our members and constantly structure the organization to meet them as fully as possible. 0———5———10

6. Our organization not only permits but encourages everyone to communicate with everyone else and insists that this occur across functional, ethnic, and any other divisions. 0———5———10

7. We expect conflict to be helpful, expect it to be openly expressed, and train our members in effective conflict resolution techniques. 0———5———10

8. We have an affirmative program that empowers members of minority groups, women, and the disabled to express their own goals and to work to achieve them. 0———5———10

Which of these should you work on? Once again, look at the visual profile you've created, then use it to select one or two items from the following list to begin working on. Let me warn you, though, that if you've rated your organization low on one or more elements, the cure for it will be neither quick nor simple. Nor will I be able to offer many specific suggestions; you'll have to find many of your basic resources outside this book.

1. *If your organization hasn't taken positive steps to ensure that all positions, to the very highest levels, are open to everyone.* The kind of creativity this book describes cannot exist in an organization that has not systematically removed the barriers to full contributions by *everyone.* I suggest that you put this issue close to the top of your "to do" list and start working on it immediately. You might want to begin by reading Roosevelt Thomas's *Beyond Race and Gender,* one of the more trustworthy books on the issue.

2. *If you have limited yourself to a narrow, "multicultural" understanding of diversity.* Reread this chapter carefully, then read Roosevelt Thomas's book. When you have a full understanding of diversity, communicate it to those in your organization who have formal responsibility for diversity and see that they begin to

communicate it broadly through the organization. Prepare yourself; it won't happen quickly—and you'll probably step on some very entrenched toes in the process.

3. *If you do not actively communicate to all your members at all levels that they are important players, essential to the success of the organization.* Ow! This is Management 101. An organization limits itself unduly when it doesn't believe and communicate this, and the limitations rise exponentially when the organization attempts to deal with diversity and to be creative. Get your head on straight on this matter, then begin communicating it to everyone you deal with. If you manage professionals like engineers or attorneys, by the way, they may resent any suggestion that support personnel are as important as they are. That simply makes the basic problem stickier—it doesn't change it.

4. *If you don't ensure that everyone focuses on organizational goals and the objectives required to achieve them.* Changing your organization from a focus on requirements and procedures to a focus on goals and objectives requires a major effort. Chapters 2 and 3 have already dealt with this; you might want to reread them as a way of getting started. Then find an experienced consultant to work with your organization to make the change.

5. *If you do not accept the validity of the individual goals and needs of all your members and constantly structure the organization to meet them as fully as possible.* Part of the mythology of traditional hierarchical organizations is that individuals should focus only on the corporation's needs, subordinating their own needs to them. Sounds good in theory, but you and I both know it never works in practice. You need to initiate a hard-nosed review of whose individual goals the organization recognizes and meets and of how it meets them. Then you need to expand your focus, to include progressively a broader and broader range of individual goals. For instance, you probably acknowledge and meet the goals of aggressive male college-educated managers pretty well, but how well do you meet the needs of single parents, who likely make up a large percentage of your clerical work force?

6. *If your organization doesn't encourage everyone to communicate with everyone else and insist that this occur across functional, ethnic, and any other divisional lines.* The natural tendency of hierarchical

organizations to limit communication to formal upward and downward channels becomes devastating when combined with the natural tendency for different functional and ethnic groups to avoid communicating with others different from themselves. Go back to the suggestion for this item in Chapter 3 and follow it. That, at least, is a beginning.

7. *If you don't accept that conflict can be helpful, expect it to be openly expressed, and train your members in effective conflict resolution techniques.* Again, traditional hierarchical organizations are not just poor but miserable at this. If yours remains stuck in that mold, brace yourself for a long and arduous haul. Start by opening up communication and getting some reliable training for your key people in conflict recognition and resolution. You'll probably find that opening up communication will bring to the surface an uncomfortable level of existing conflict. When you accept and resolve this conflict, you facilitate a further opening of communication (which will bring to the surface a deeper level of existing conflict, which leads to the need for more conflict resolution skills, and so on in an ascending virtuous cycle).

8. *If you lack an affirmative program that empowers members of minority groups, women, and the disabled to express their own goals and to work to achieve them.* Our society in general and many organizations in particular communicate to individuals in these groups that they are less than competent to achieve their own goals and that they must be helped by wiser and more powerful organization-appointed EEO officials or self-appointed representatives of their group. You cannot help people become more effective by taking the responsibility to decide what is best for them and how it should be achieved out of their hands. You can, however, help them in significant ways to empower themselves and to speak for themselves. While this takes a well-thought-out program in the long run, you can begin with a simple action. Communicate to all your managers how important it is to be sensitive to each individual as an individual and to listen insightfully to what the individual says. If your managers lack strong skills at listening insightfully, there are courses available to help them develop such skills.

Chapter 5

Do Creativity and Technology Require a Shotgun Marriage?

The basic imperative of the computational infrastructure is to push toward the day when, for humans, there is no more business as usual.

—Walter Kiechel III

Or, as Brenda Laurel put much the same thought:

Life is too short to beat the hell out of yourself doing something that should take a quarter of the time and be an order of magnitude more fun.

For most of us, the announcement "We're getting a new computer system" is almost as exciting as a trip to the dentist. We spend all too much of our working days feeding data into these systems, working around their glitches, then trying to wrestle some tidbit of useful information out of them in time to do some good. Is technology, particularly computer technology, the natural enemy of creativity, or can it be used in ways that enhance creativity? If it can be, how do you do it? This chapter explores these questions.

Two Basic Principles of Successful Technology

Let me begin by sharing with you two straightforward principles. You know the first, though you may not practice it (many companies don't). You may not be familiar with the second, but you should be. Whether you intend to have a constantly creative organization or not, if you take these two principles seriously you will prevent at least half the disappointments common to users of new technology.

Strategy First, All Else Next

Organizations that use technology effectively use it first to support their strategic goals. That sounds obvious, doesn't it? But do most organizations, including your own:

- Start with a strategic business need rather than a sexy new technology (such as client-server architecture or multimedia)?
- Design the technology to align with the organization's culture and basic systems rather than implement the technology and then adapt the organization to it?
- Ask throughout the process how the new technology will affect customer service instead of implementing potentially irritating technology like voice messaging as a knee-jerk response to personnel costs?

I could go on and on. From what I read, most companies seem to focus their automation efforts on internal concerns—on cost containment, inventory efficiency, and ever increasing controls. Not that computer systems can't help with these; they can, of course. Not that they're not important; they are. But unless these uses are carefully tied to strategic goals, and specifically to long-term customer satisfaction and profitability, you may be building an ever more sophisticated dinosaur. The alternative, a turbocharged Jaguar with a few scratches on its paint and a few lumps in its seat, seems clearly preferable.

But, as I said, you know that, don't you?

And Then There's Grudin's Law

You may not have heard of Grudin's Law. It goes like this:

> When those who benefit are not those who do the
> work, then the technology is likely to fail or, at least,
> be subverted.[1]

Here's an example from my own experience. For the last several years, organizations have been attempting to use "artificial intelligence," and particularly expert systems, to make their operations more efficient and effective. An internal consultant with a large systems design activity proposed to apply expert systems to the organization's help desk. In her view, systems design could identify the expertise the help-desk personnel applied to resolve the really sticky problems and put it in an expert system. Then the system would be available to provide answers, regardless of the motivation or skill of the human beings involved.

The suggestion never got off the ground. It flatly violated Grudin's Law. The expert system presumably would have been helpful to help-desk customers and to management. In the way it was proposed, however, it provided no benefit whatsoever to the help-desk staff. To them, it said "You do some really neat things, so we're going to take everything that makes your job interesting and skilled and let the computer do it." Is it any wonder that the people who would have used the system found reason after reason to oppose it from the beginning?

Unfortunately, contemporary organizations make this mistake again and again and again. Companies typically design and implement computer systems without regard for Grudin's Law. Skilled clerks are turned into data input clerks; technicians are turned into machine tenders whose only function is to turn the machine off if it malfunctions and get someone else to fix it; even managers may be expected to follow a rigid automated system when making decisions.[2]

Grudin's Law is so important that I want to use another example, one particularly relevant to the last point in the previous paragraph. Several firms and individuals (myself included) have designed decision support software that helps individuals make systematic decisions. We have good evidence that the use of such a program will lead to better, more consistent decisions. But every program (again, my own included) has been a commercial flop. Why? Because each of us knows that we make good decisions; it's *other* people who make the poor decisions. In the case of the automated decision support system used by managers (mentioned in the preceding paragraph), it was unilaterally imposed by the CEO of the corporation. It may last until the day he leaves, but quite possibly not one day longer.[3]

In sum, you will minimize your chance of having new technology fail if you follow one simple precept, based on Grudin's Law:

> Design every system so that there is a clear payoff for those who must operate it, not just for those who use its results.

Is this difficult? Of course it is, though the rest of this chapter will offer you some help in doing it. If you don't do it, however, you will quite possibly try to implement a system doomed from the beginning. Even worse, you may try to implement one that comes close enough to working that it drains resources year after year as it supporters valiantly try to make it succeed. Paying close attention to strategic goals and to Grudin's Law will help you avoid or at least minimize the pitfalls of these systems. So will the other principles in this chapter.

How to Combine Creativity and Technology

As Donald Norman keeps pointing out, we design most systems—and especially computer-based systems—backward. We look for what can be automated, automate it, then give what's left to the humans in the system. The result? Humans are often forced to perform detailed, exacting, repetitive work—precisely the kind of work that most of us do poorly! Norman has put this quite succinctly:

> When technology is not designed from a human-centered point of view, it doesn't reduce the incidence of

human error nor minimize the impact when errors do occur.

Yes, people do indeed err. Therefore the technology should be designed to take this well-known fact into account. . . .

The trick in designing technology is to provide situations that minimize error, that minimize the impact of error, and that maximize the chance of discovering error once it has been committed.[4]

As long as systems are designed by concentrating on what the machinery can do and then delegating the rest to humans, they will underutilize those humans and assign them tasks at which they are prone to error. And they will subvert even the best-intentioned efforts to develop a creative organization. GE spent tremendous sums on technology in the 1980s, but in some cases has taken it out of its factories. Why? "GE's big breakthrough has been giving workers flexibility and unprecedented authority to decide how to do their work."[5] The Saturn Corporation deliberately chose a "mid-tech" approach to its Tennessee plant, relying instead on independent work teams to produce high-quality cars. It worked in spades. In both these cases, the companies had to turn away from supposedly high-tech solutions because their machine-centered design interfered with the flexible, creative work force the companies needed.

Is there an alternative? Most definitely, but it involves some serious frame bending and breaking. The conviction that machines should be maximized and humans fitted in is one of the most deeply grooved frames in American business and industry. There are other, more effective frames; because they're not as deeply embedded in our culture, they're not as neat and simple as machine-centered design. But they exist, and they work. More exactly, design principles do exist that will enable an organization to make the best use of both its humans and its technology and, specifically, to use technology in a way that directly supports creativity. (I'm focusing here on automating processes; however, the principles apply to a wide range of technologies.)

These are three of the basic principles:

1. Before automating any process, analyze it carefully and reengineer it before automating it.
2. Delegate repetitive work to the technology. When you cannot feasibly accomplish this, outsource the repetitive work.
3. Analyze the remaining work as a whole. First determine what can best be done by humans; then determine what can best be done by machines; and then allocate the remaining work between humans and computers. You will probably have to cycle through this step two or more times to get the best balance between humans and their computerized fellow.

Now, let's see what each of these principles really means.

Analyze and Reengineer

From the publicity reengineering has gotten lately, you'd think that we just discovered it. Not so. The basic principles of reengineering apparently have to be rediscovered at least once each decade; I was reading authors in the early 1970s who were stressing it then. And they had their own horror stories, just as we do today.

Despite the impression you may get from books, magazines, and many consultants, reengineering isn't just for major organizational face-lifts. In fact, you can get much the same benefits by applying it consistently to smaller projects—without the organizational trauma that usually accompanies major reengineering. (Let me warn you, though; a thorough analysis of a small project often leads directly to the need for reengineering on a much broader level.)

Reengineering is based on one simple, basic, and unpleasant fact: *Any process that remains in place for a period of time will become inefficient.* The inefficiency isn't just global. It reflects itself in each individual job as well. Within the last several months, two different organizational consultants I know have told me about work situations they've analyzed in which no more than 15 percent of the time of engineers (in one case) and managers (in the other) was spent on true value-adding duties. When I remarked on this to a friend, his response was: "They're lucky that it's even that high." (As I recall, he mentioned a figure of 8 percent as typical.) Various authors over the past several years have noted that when a system is reengineered before it's automated the reengineering typically results in greater increases in efficiency than the automation does (which may still be very helpful itself).[6]

With the emphasis on major corporate reengineering, it's easy to forget that every time a process action team improves a process or practice it engages in reengineering. Just as you will make more progress on the whole from a series of small reengineering projects, so will you make more progress if the reengineering is done by the players involved in the process. When necessary, their efforts can be augmented by outside specialists, who function as consultants, but never as "the experts." The more that individuals work together to reengineer the processes that directly affect them, the greater the potential they will develop for creative action in every aspect of their job.

Remember that the goal of a constantly creative organization is everyday creativity, a way of operating in which creativity is so deeply ingrained that it is "nothing special." Reengineering processes and improving practices, with or without automation, is a key part of this creativity.

A final thought. Some managers may be troubled by the thought of delegating the authority to "mess with" processes to their operators, many of whom may be unskilled and working for minimum wage. If you're one of them, you may or may not be reassured to know that they're doing it already. Most workers don't simply follow procedures (though if you ask them, they'll tell you they do). Instead, they find shortcuts and time and effort savers, which they share with one another. For the most part, they do this without training and without regard for whether their modifications pay off for the company (remember Ben and Dale). Teaching them basic improvement tools, guiding them to help the company at the same time as they help themselves, and seeing that their efforts earn recognition and extra income builds on a practice already in place. Think about that.

Let the Technology Do the Grunt Work

Unfortunately, the traditional machine-centered approach to technology implementation often removes not only creativity but also skill and interest from the job. That approach also generates a particularly vicious circle. It creates jobs that can be held by unskilled, low-paid workers—because the organization is trying to control costs or compensate for a lack of skilled and motivated workers, or both. Because the jobs are unskilled and uninteresting, the company attracts unskilled, unmotivated workers. These workers drive the firm to deskill jobs further, which attracts more unskilled, unmotivated workers . . . and the cycle continues. As more than one person has noted, American schools are currently producing precisely the unskilled, unmotivated graduates that American business and industry forecast a decade ago it would need.[7]

Does this seem overstated? Consider the conclusions of Barbara Garson in the book *The Electronic Sweatshop* (published in 1988). After visiting site after site that had been automated, she concluded:

> The one thing I didn't anticipate was the underlying motive. I had assumed that employers automate in order to cut costs. And, indeed, cost cutting is often the result. But I discovered in the course of this research that neither the designers nor the users of the highly centralized technology I was seeing knew much about its costs and benefits, its bottom-line efficiency. The specific form that automation is taking seems to be based less on a rational desire for profit than on an irrational prejudice against people.[8]

Is this too extreme? Consider these words by Shoshana Zuboff in her highly acclaimed book *In the Age of the Smart Machine*:

> Imagine the following scenario: Intelligence is lodged in the smart machine at the expense of the human capacity for critical judgment. Organizational members become ever more dependent, docile, and secretly cynical. As more tasks must be accomplished through the medium of information technology (I call this "computer-mediated work"), the sentient body loses its salience as a source of knowledge, resulting in profound disorienta-

tion and loss of meaning. People intensify their search for avenues of escape through drugs, apathy, or adversarial conflict, as the majority of jobs in our offices and factories become increasingly isolated, remote, routine, and perfunctory.[9]

Nothing will derail any movement toward a creative organization more quickly than this approach. If a creative organization is your goal, you must reverse the traditional priorities. See that your automated systems perform the dull, repetitive work. See that the remaining work is interesting and provides the opportunity for its performers to develop skills useful to you and to them and to exercise their creativity.

This approach will permit you to attract and retain workers with greater skills and motivation. Even more, it will save you from having to hire and hold unskilled workers in dead-end jobs.

Let me dwell on that for just a moment. Organizations are so accustomed to dozens, hundreds, or even thousands of low-skilled, low-paid workers that they often don't bother to think about their impact. If what you want is a routine, by-the-numbers work force producing an acceptable product or service, you don't have to worry about it either. But if you want a highly creative, highly competitive organization based on high performance, you don't want unskilled workers. You want skilled performers, able to contribute effectively in a rapidly changing, highly innovative environment. You literally can't afford low-wage, low-skilled workers.

So replace them with technology wherever you can. Let the technology do the grunt work so that your human performers can handle the challenging tasks, particularly those that require quick responses to unpredictable situations and people. In case this sounds idealistic, or even difficult, let me give you a few quick examples:

• A MAJOR HOME IMPROVEMENT CHAIN found that customers wanted assistance in designing decks, but that employees skilled enough to provide any real assistance were few and far between. It contracted for a computer-based design system that allowed even new sales clerks to input customer needs and end up with a detailed design, bill of materials included. Increased productivity was the primary goal, and the chain achieved it. It also significantly improved employee satisfaction, because even new employees were now able genuinely to help customers.[10]

• FEDERAL EXPRESS's DADS system computerizes package pickup and delivery. The reduction in paperwork frees frontline people to concentrate on dealing with their customers, and in the process makes the job more interesting and challenging. When Marshall Field developed a highly automated point-of-sale system, the department store also intended to make its sales personnel more effective and to allow them to concentrate on customers. In the process, of course, their jobs also became more challenging.[11]

• It's remarkable how few SUPERMARKETS AND DISCOUNT STORES have figured out how their checkers' jobs could be changed. Virtually every one of these stores now has bar code readers at their checkout stands, augmented by electronic registers that compute the correct change. From the point of view of many, perhaps most, of these stores, this has simply deskilled an already low-skilled job. Almost none of them seem to have caught on that automation could free the checker to be the primary customer satisfaction person in the store. It seems clear that they're missing a source of meaningful competitive advantage.

The point? Even traditional automation doesn't have to deskill jobs; it can change the role of the performer to a more challenging and positive one. And even traditional automation can free performers from previously boring jobs to concentrate on customer service.

But what about the unskilled jobs that can't be automated away? If they contribute significant value to the customer, find a way to enrich them. (TQM can be helpful here.) If they don't contribute value, *outsource them*. Just don't waste potentially creative managers on routine, low-skilled operations.[12]

To Each His/Her/Its Own

Now we come to the key point: If you want technology to support creativity, organize technology so that computers do what they do best and let humans do what they do best. This way they reinforce one another and build on one another's strengths.

Does that sound strange? But isn't this the way that we try to organize human combinations, so that they build on the strengths of their members and compensate for their weaknesses? Why should we treat the combination of people and computers differently?

In short, the most effective design treats humans and computers as *partners*, each doing what he/she/it does best and compensating for what the other cannot do as well.

Granted, this sound nice—but how do you accomplish it? Even more, how do you accomplish it in such a way that the system supports human creativity? I've already said that there are no a-b-c procedures, but there are some very clear guidelines. First, don't begin by asking "What can the machine do for us here?"—the traditional machine-centered approach. Instead, start with this very different question: "In what circumstances do people produce the highest level of performance?" We have some very specific answers to this question. Individuals perform at their highest level when they have:

- Clear goals defined by practical standards and supported by useful feedback
- A sense of direct engagement with the work, which presents "a continual feeling of challenge, one that is neither so difficult as to create a sense of hopelessness and frustration nor so easy as to produce boredom"[13]
- "Appropriate tools that fit the user and task so well that they aid and do not distract" from direct involvement with the work[14]
- Freedom from any other distractions that break the continuity of involvement with the work
- The autonomy to control the key factors of success, supported by a nonblaming organizational environment
- A sense that the goal is sufficiently worthwhile that the time and attention spent on the job do not seem wasted

This leads to the next question. Once we know what people need to achieve a high-level performance, how can we use computers effectively to support this performance? Fortunately, if we use both computers and humans in the ways that each is most efficient, we will end up supporting high-level performance for both.

We have learned a great deal about the comparative strengths and weaknesses of humans and computers. We know that computers will outperform humans when the tasks:

- Are stable and require high-speed, very accurate computation
- Are repetitive
- Require remembering and/or finding stable, clearly defined information
- Involve the application of clear, stable rules to large numbers of cases

Computers can also outperform humans in situations where human emotions may interfere with reaching the correct decision. A major credit card issuer found, for instance, that a system built to advise representatives whether to grant credit in a specific situation was more accurate than the representatives themselves. Automated stock-market systems also tend to make more accurate decisions in many circumstances than most individuals do.[15]

On the other hand, we also know that computers do not deal well with:

- Changing situations
- Ill-defined (fuzzy) situations
- Situations that require effective responses to conditions that cannot be defined in advance
- Situations that require effective interpersonal relationships
- Situations in which emotion plays a helpful part (such as those requiring an individual to "go the extra mile" or requiring active compassion to establish relationships and goals)

Note, by the way, that these are basically the situations that increasingly characterize companies in highly competitive markets *and* are the conditions that constantly creative organizations deal with most effectively.

Now that you have the answers to the two key questions, you can take a straightforward approach. Look at the tasks to be performed—after they and the process they're part of have been reengineered, of course. Give the tasks that humans do best and that support high-level performance to the humans and design the computer system to support them. Then give the remaining tasks, most of which humans would find boring and at which they are error-prone, to the computer.

Don't forget that the goal is to create an interactive human-computer system that enhances the effectiveness and creativity of the humans and uses computers in ways that will best support their effectiveness and creativity. The design guidelines I have set forth are a start toward this goal, but hardly a detailed prescription for systems development. You and your systems designers need to understand the principles, use them to analyze your situation—and then respond to it creatively.

Preserving Your Core Competence

One last point. Computer systems can detract from the competence an organization requires to compete in two very different ways. Traditional computer systems do this by requiring the people who use them to substitute systems knowledge for the underlying subject-matter knowledge.

Here's an example of how this happens. You're being briefed with data from one of your systems. The briefing starts out dealing with the subject matter: the need to control inventory, move supplies through the system, or track merit raises. Someone asks why a particular total is so high; there's an uncomfortable pause while the briefer consults another specialist, who then explains the elements that make up the total.

What happened? The briefer has just demonstrated something that most people who deal with systems take for granted: that the knowledge of how to feed the system, how to get around it, how to make it work despite glitches, and how to understand its output becomes more important than the knowledge of the subject matter itself. Your expert performers are now experts in maintaining the computer system, but they are no longer expert at managing the underlying subject-matter processes that the systems supposedly are serving. Ask the human resources specialist how college prospects are entered into and tracked through the system and she can tell you without hesitation. Ask her how valid the criteria are on the basis of which selections are made and you will most likely get a hesitant answer, if any answer at all.

Why? Because human beings can hold and use only a limited amount of information at one time. When an individual must give time and attention to the automated system, he can't spend that same time and attention on the subject-matter knowledge of his field. In these circumstances, the individual and the organization both lose. The system simply demands too much expert knowledge to run. The competence needed by the company is diminished.

Two decades ago, when central processor time and storage were precious, there was at least some excuse (though never a good one) for maximizing the system. With today's technology, there is no excuse. We saw in the previous section that high-performance organizations require appropriate tools that fit the user and task so well that they aid rather than distract from direct involvement with the work. An automated system, no matter how extensive, should be a tool. Those who use it should do so almost effortlessly, like a skilled carpenter using a plane. Your computer folks will tell you that it's damnably difficult and time-consuming to create such systems. They're right. You just have to decide which is more important to you: effective, creative people or overly rigid, inappropriate machinery that in effect becomes the master of these same creative people. You cannot have both.

The second way in which computer systems can diminish competence is far more difficult to control. Let's say that you want to give high-competence tasks to your human performers to develop their skills and creativity, but that qualified individuals can't be hired, trained, or retained to perform the work. In this situation, it's terribly tempting to use newer technologies like expert systems or neural networks that allow the computer to perform the tasks. For some functions, such as inventory control, credit, or even some help-desk support, this works. But be careful just what you offload onto the computer. Remember this rule:

> The more essential an activity is for the long-term success of the organization, the more it should be retained by human performers.

You do not *ever* want to get into a situation where the critical skills for organizational success reside in computer systems that can be updated only by staff specialists or external contractors. Put your human firepower where the action is; hold on to your human expertise in that area no matter what. Then design whatever computer systems it takes to support this expertise.

What to Do Now

Organizations differ dramatically in the kind and amount of technology they use. So, instead of asking you to begin by rating your organization's use of technology, I'm simply going to outline four steps that will be useful to almost any organization.

1. Inventory the computer-based systems used by your organization; if the organization is large, inventory the major systems. Slot every system into one of three categories:

- *Frontline systems* are those that directly affect service to the customer. These systems might include a help desk to answer customer questions; an on-line order system in customer offices; or a voice-messaging system that your customers contact when they call in. If you have a limited number of important suppliers, count systems with which they directly interface in this category.
- *Direct-support systems* do not directly interface with the customer but directly support customer-focused activities. Such systems include automated inventory systems; accounts receivable and billing systems; and sale support systems.

• *Internal systems* are the systems that automate the organization's internal processes, such as a cost-accounting system; an inventory system for consumable supplies; or a
contract-tracking system.

2. Frontline systems are obviously the most important. However, instead of focusing on them, take another step first. Look at
every system in every category and ask this question about it: Is
there anything in the operation of this system that impairs our
ability to respond to our customers? Whenever you get a yes, put
that system at the top of your list to be revised or even eliminated.
Then do what has to be done to change the system, or at least to
work around it until it can be changed.

3. Then do a priority check, based on the results of the first
step. Are the frontline and direct-support systems the ones that
are getting the attention? Are they the ones slated to be upgraded
first? Is someone looking for new ways that systems can be used
to increase customer service? If you start getting noes to these
questions, the organization's priorities for its systems are mis-
guided; they need to be changed.

4. Now we get to the step critical to a constantly creative
organization. You want to identify and then change each of these
three situations:

• *What systems force individual players to perform repetitive, unskilled, or low-skilled work, and particularly work requiring a
high level of accuracy?* Common forms of such work are data
input, machine tending of rapid, repetitive processes, or
review of documents for the presence of easily identified
data. If the systems can be changed to automate these
tasks, do it. If they cannot, outsource the tasks if possible.
Remember, every time one of your players must perform
this type of work, you have deprived that individual of the
chance to contribute to the overall creativity of your organization.
• *What systems require players to have special skills in using the
system, such as knowing undocumented input requirements,
work-arounds, or the meaning of unclear outputs?* When you

discover these, create a working list. You will not be able to solve these problems in weeks or even months, especially when these are basic organizational systems. Every time a change is made, however, press to see that the system is upgraded to make it easier for humans to use. You don't want to waste precious organizational creativity on figuring out how to make machine-centered systems perform properly despite themselves.

- *Finally, what skills and knowledge important to the organization are being offloaded from humans onto systems?* Payroll systems have generally transferred abilities from humans to computers. Because payroll know-how is a generalized knowledge, with little or no effect on competition, this seldom does serious harm. But have you started installing systems that take competencies key to competitive success away from human performers? Are these systems now maintained and updated by staff specialists or contractors because they are the only ones with the knowledge? *Reverse this trend now!*

A Final Thought

Much of this chapter may have sounded a little unusual, perhaps a lot so. But remember, we're not trying to design conventional automated systems. Our goal is to create and maintain a constantly creative organization—and to design the automated systems needed to support that goal. Because the overwhelming majority of automated systems have been designed to maximize the machine rather than the human, conventional design criteria just don't work well in a creative organization. If you want a constantly creative organization, you'll have to design systems creatively. And you can.

Chapter 6

How Can You Have Creativity, Reliability, and Efficiency?

An organization that runs like clockwork is great—but only if its goal is to run around in the same circles forever.

—Anonymous

Regularity, repeatability, and efficiency have been the watchwords of American industry for most of this century. And not just American industry. The Japanese ask for more creativity and contribution from their line workers than American companies do, but direct this creativity into improving ways of implementing and improving processes—that are repeated again and again. How can an organization square creativity with the need for reliability and efficiency? In this chapter, I suggest some answers to that question.

Creativity and Discipline

Many people, and perhaps you're one, believe that creativity means self-indulgence and lack of discipline. After all, many creative people dress weirdly; a friend of mine once called systems programmers (a necessarily creative group) the "long hair and sandals group." Look at the extravagant lives of some artists: Van Gogh cutting off his ear, the on- and off-stage exploits of many rock groups. And look at the creative people in all too many organizations, spending time on what interests them, not on what needs to be done.

Chapter 1 stressed "Focused Creativity," and the word *focused* is the key. The Van Goghs, and even the Van Halens, of the world practice focused creativity. Someone once remarked to Charlie Pride, the country and western singer, that he had been extremely lucky. "I certainly have," Pride replied, "and, you know, the harder I've worked the luckier I've been." Individuals who are both focused and creative, that is, those who are successful, are extraordinarily disciplined people. They often seem strange to others precisely because of the demands of their discipline; they simply don't have time and energy to spend on many of the everyday concerns the rest of us focus on.

If I may, let me give you a personal example. This is my sixth book. When you hear that, what mental image do you get? A practiced author sitting down and typing out a smooth flow of words? Nice thought! I spend at least as much time now reworking whatever I write as I did when I was creating my first book. I think I've improved as a writer, but my ability to view my work critically has improved right along with it. I see problems now that were invisible to me five, or even two, books ago.

To the best of my knowledge, almost everyone who attempts to be creative in any field has much the same experience. We try continually to improve what we do, to make it at least a little better than last time—and this leaves us little time to waste following rabbit trails into the underbrush. We may in fact try something new that fails, because creative work requires constant experimentation (remember Chapter 1), but few of us do it simply because it looks interesting.

In short and emphatically, creativity and discipline need not be mortal enemies. They are not even rivals. When creativity is focused and its successful use rewarded, discipline comes as part of the package.

Creativity and Routine Work

The real problem raised by creativity has nothing to do with discipline. The real problem is routine work. Creative people and routine, repetitive work *are* often mortal enemies.

Yet doesn't routine, repetitive work have to be done? Yes, it does, at least in most organizations. Yes, it does, but it can be reduced. That's why in Chapter 5 I recommended so strongly that this type of work be delegated to computers or contracted out; constant routine work suffocates humans who intend to be creative.

Note that I said "constant." Even the most creative among us—people like Edwin Land or Bill Gates—don't spend all their time being creative. A certain amount of routine activity serves as a balance to the tension and stress of really creative work. Good job design takes account of this and tries to balance the two in individual jobs. (See Chapter 7 for more on this.)

More important, we can't discuss creative and routine work in a vacuum. Both exist in an organizational context, specifically in the context of the innovation cycle, so we need to look at this cycle.[1]

The Innovation Cycle

Most innovations develop through a cycle that has six relatively distinct phases: discovery, development, implementation, production, improvement, and elaboration. The six phases shade into each other, but each is distinct from the others. And these phases characterize innovation in any field: Newtonian physics, Baroque music, single-lens reflex cameras, total quality management, mutual funds—you name it. Because the cycle is so universal, understanding it can help a creative organization be efficient in the right way.

Discovery

Discovery kicks off the cycle. Someone makes a technological breakthrough (the laser), discovers a new process (TQM), gets an idea for a new service (Federal Express), thinks up a new form for adhesives (Post-it notes), or simply devises a new way to use E-mail. The idea sounds neat, perhaps even feels great.

We generally identify creativity with this step, the "aha!" moment. Creativity does inspire aha!'s, often the specific kind of aha! that comes from bending or breaking an organization's existing frames. Someone "jumps outside" the ordinary way of looking at things. Imagine manufacturing a note with adhesive that could be pulled loose easily; who'd ever think of such a thing?!

Discovery requires *scouts*, individuals who keep looking beyond the current situation toward a new one. Sometimes a scout looks toward distant mountains, estimating the time and effort required to reach them. Sometimes he or she simply sees more in the immediate situation than others can: a path along the hill or the signs of a spring in what looks to everyone else like a barren patch of ground. Whether scouts look far or near, they make the discovery and point the direction that kicks off the innovation process.

Development

Development determines whether the aha! discovery will ever see the light of day. In the case of major products or services, hundreds, perhaps thousands, of sticky problems have to be solved. Even with small discoveries—say, how to process an order in half the time—dozens of details may have to be ironed out.

Sometimes the problems are overcome, sometimes the problems win. At the end of World War II, forecasters confidently predicted that there would be a TV in every home and a helicopter in every garage. Now we all have TVs, but not helicopters. Twenty years later, automation and management by objectives (MBO) were going to revolutionize American business and industry. Automation has, MBO is passé. Videoconferencing has been forecast to revolutionize meetings for more than a decade now; it hasn't yet. Sometimes the problems are overcome, sometimes the problems win—and it happens in this phase.

Development requires two talents: that of the *designer* and that of the *critic*. The best designers are also their own best critics, so sufficiently talented individuals can perform both roles. More commonly, the roles are differentiated, with some performers working as designers to give shape to the vision, while others serve as critics, winnowing out the false trails and mediocre solutions. In well-functioning organizations, individuals and groups switch easily from one role to the other, so that both always understand the need for both.

Implementation

If the idea survives this far, now it actually gets embodied out there somewhere. If it's a product, everything has to be set up to manufacture it—not to mention advertise, distribute, and service it. If it's a service, the demands are just as pressing. Even if nothing more is involved than a small change in an internal practice, the day has to come when it's done the new way. Only then do we find out for sure whether it was worth the effort or not.

In implementation, the *impresario* takes over from the designer/critic. Impresarios understand what it takes, and whom it takes, to bring the developed discovery into the real world and make it practical. They know how to pull the technologies and the people together to make things work. Designers and critics may not always meet deadlines; impresarios always do. To draft an old metaphor, when the rubber meets the road the impresarios make certain it rolls.

Production

When we think of routine and efficiency, we normally think of the production phase. The company climbs the learning curve, producing its product or service more cost-effectively day by day and month by month. The same thing happens with practices and processes; they have to be learned and then practiced with as little waste motion as possible. Up to this point, the new idea was pure cost; now the payback begins.

Here *technicians* step to the front. They understand how to fine-tune the practices and processes that produce the goods and services. They balance out the machines and the people, track and control the costs, measure the market penetration, clean the metaphorical but irritating sand out of the metaphorical gears, and perform the dozens of other functions required to maintain a going business.

Improvement

In a highly competitive world, this phase begins almost as soon as production does. On the one hand, the company improves the product or service; the major software companies begin work on the next version long before the current version hits the market. On the other, if an organization practices *kaizen* (constant process improvement), it begins improving its production practices and processes as soon as they are in place.

Improvement requires *students*. Technicians all too often become prisoners of the current situation, absorbed by the fire underfoot and the alligator crawling down the bank. Students try to find a piece of high ground from which they can take a broader look around. Students want to know who's starting the fires, what's attracting the alligators, and—most of all—how to do something about it.

Elaboration

Elaboration is the final phase and, all too often, the longest one. In this phase, everyone becomes a *tinkerer*. The tinkerer fiddles with the product or service: tailfins get higher, seven new varieties of money-market funds are marketed, presentations are fancied up endlessly with the latest graphics packages. (I'll bet most units in your organization use fancy fax forms, and probably modify them every few weeks or months, even though ornate forms cost far more to send than simple ones.)

How can you tell the student from the tinkerer, improvement from elaboration? Improvement adds value to the customer by providing new benefits and to the company by reducing costs or raising margins. Elaboration changes the product or service, practice or process, without adding meaningful value for anyone. It's more interesting; unfortunately, no one but the tinkerers care.

Reliability and Creativity

If we use the innovation cycle as a lens to focus on how companies function, it perhaps sheds some new light on the question of reliability and efficiency. Our ideas of these come from "mature" industries, such as the automobile industry was thought to be in the fifties and sixties. In such an industry, discovery and development are sharply limited, implementation is repetitive, improvement is infrequent, and elaboration is carried out systematically through marginal improvements in features and design changes for the sake of design changes.

That leaves production—and our basic ideas of reliability and efficiency derive specifically from long-run production processes. Nor do these have to be physical processes. Credit card companies and banks process millions of pieces of paper each month on a pink-collar assembly line. When a company does the same thing thousands or millions of times each month, it must ensure that each repetition is as waste-free as possible.

Here you have the first key to reconciling creativity and efficiency: In our fast-changing world, the production phase is being absorbed by the implementation phase at one end and by the improvement phase at the other. Instead of production runs of thousands, an increasing number of companies today have runs of only hundreds or dozens. The National Bicycle Industrial Company of Japan produces bikes successfully in lots of one.[2] Health insurance firms tailor packages to individual clients; different plans are similar but never exactly alike. There are so many technologies for training that a training designer could go an entire working life without ever producing two courses delivered in exactly the same way.

When production runs become shorter and shorter and routine work is automated or contracted out, the whole meaning of efficiency and reliability changes—and changes dramatically. The rest of this chapter looks in detail at just what this change means.

Squelch Elaboration

Let's begin with one of the great historic sources of waste in organizations. Because we have concentrated so heavily on waste and inefficiency in production processes, we have ignored a virtual mountain of waste: the tendency of companies, functions, and individual performers to elaborate, elaborate, elaborate. Let me give you a few examples:

• American automakers (and many other manufacturers) were locked in a cycle of constant elaboration during the 1960s and 1970s. Some genuinely new models, such as the Mustang, were introduced, but, for the most part, it was an endless succession of sheet-metal and chrome modifications and marginal increases in functionality. The Japanese grabbed market share in the late 1970s and 1980s largely because they created new processes that enabled them to offer a genuine innovation: high quality.

• Several years ago, the cover of a major computer magazine had a graph showing the impact of presentation packages. Two lines moved across the X-axis, which represented the decade of the 1980s. One line, the attractiveness and flash, shot sharply upward. The second line, the information conveyed, trudged along on the same level. More time, more pizzazz, no more value.

• As you read this, in thousands of offices all across America (and probably around the world), individuals are elaborating the products and services they touch. Letters are rewritten endlessly, not to change the content but to tweak the style. Fax cover-sheets, brochures, newsletters, presentations, manuals—these make up only a small part of the mountain of products and services, practices and processes, that are elaborated every day.

• Worst of all, as you read this, thousands of companies all across America are valiantly struggling with their latest Flavor of the Month. Instead of beginning with a pressing business need and responding to it, they have begun with a fashionable program, confident that if they just do what this book or that consultant tells them to they will reform themselves and solve their problems. Immense amounts of time get wasted, attention is drawn away from what's needed to solve the real problems, and the cynicism level rises another few notches. Think I'm exaggerating? The *best* that can be said for major change programs like TQM, JIT, or process engineering is that companies adopting them will have at least a 30 percent chance of success.

I don't pretend to have a complete explanation for this rampant inefficiency, but I can suggest two major causes. First, performers with the desire and ability to improve what they see around them are stuck in jobs that don't make use of their creativity, so they use this creativity in the only way available to them. Second, the organization has failed to understand and to communicate the difference between improvement and elaboration, which is the difference between value to the customer or the enterprise and a series of meaningless frills. What would happen if the organization put these same bored individuals in jobs focused on customer value and gave them the necessary scope and rewards for their creativity? It would be a major step toward becoming a constantly creative organization—because it would shift a sizable amount of effort from elaboration into improvement and, probably, even discovery.

Creativity and Efficiency in Tandem

Think of your business and let's go through the cycle of innovation as you do. The cycle begins with a discovery, large or small. Then the embryo idea is fleshed out in the development period. The fleshing out may not always be exciting, but it requires, if anything, more creativity than the discovery itself. Now development gives way to implementation, and the rapidity of change in today's market requires a healthy dose of creativity here too. The production that's left after automating and outsourcing may not seem creative, but wait: The best Japanese companies have shown us how to absorb the production phase into the improvement phase, and we know that improvement requires creativity.

M'gosh, it turns out that *everything your company does requires creativity*. We can't have a problem of creativity versus reliability and efficiency; we don't have that luxury in today's marketplace. We have, however, a far more serious problem: How do you do creative work efficiently? Because we've concentrated so intently over the years on production efficiency, we're only beginning to realize that efficient creativity can be an issue. Despite that, any organization can take specific steps to ensure that its operations are as efficient and reliable as possible at each stage of the innovation process.

Efficient Discovery

To understand what efficiency and reliability mean for discovery, we have to understand the goal of discovery. Simply stated, it is to produce a constant string of new ideas for products, services, practices, and processes—all relevant to the organization's strategy.

For many companies, discovery means an R&D department. I'm not necessarily talking about R&D departments, though, when I talk about discovery. You quite possibly don't even have a formal department, and that's not necessarily a drawback. I've always liked the approach of Gordon Forward, founder of Chaparral Steel:

> [W]e've tried to bring research into the factory and make it a line function. We make the people who are producing the steel responsible for keeping their process on the leading edge of technology worldwide. If they have to travel, they travel. If they have to figure out what the next step is, they go out and visit where people are doing interesting things. . . . *The lab is the plant.*[3]

If that approach will work in a steel minimill—and Chaparral is a very successful company—what can you do in an organization built on creative knowledge work? Everything. This is the first lesson for reliability and efficiency at the discovery level: Get everyone involved in discovery. Expect everyone—whether they do development, implementation, production, or improvement—to be scouts.

The second lesson comes from Chapters 3 and 4: Keep the interactions in the company as diverse as possible. This includes cultural diversity, of course. But it also includes functional diversity (product developers, programmers, human resources specialists, marketers, and so on). See that players from different backgrounds and points of view talk constantly with one another. The greatest enemy of discovery within a company is framelock, and constant communication among unlike individuals is your best defense against framelock.

Look back at the list of the characteristics of an organization good at flexible framing described in Chapter 3. Each of these also characterizes an organization that is efficient and reliable at the discovery phase.

To sum it all up: The better you are at keeping your frames flexible, the more efficient and reliable you will be at discovering new products, services, practices, and processes.

Efficient Development

When most people think of creativity, they think of discovery. Certainly discovery has a level of flash possessed by no other phase of the innovation process. The development phase often gets little attention, but it demands at least as much creativity. At this phase, however, creativity must be combined with hard, often detailed work. Even more important, creativity must operate in tandem with highly developed critical abilities; designers need critics. Why? The goal of discovery was to produce a variety of ideas; the goal of development is to refine these ideas, weed out those that can't be made practical, and bring out every iota of value in the ones that have the sweet smell of success about them.

What do efficiency and reliability mean in the development phase? First of all, the phase is both efficient and reliable when it produces products, services, practices, and processes that (1) are ready for implementation and (2) have a high probability of success. While both frame bending and the use of diversity and conflict remain important in this phase, the dominant quality required is that of *enthusiastic objectivity*.

Objectivity is the synthesis of three qualities identified in Chapter 3: telling it like it really is, encouraging everyone to communicate with everyone else, and focusing on the merits of an idea, not on personalities and power structures. Although these qualities support organizational creativity in general, they particularly support the development phase. If a good idea is rejected or a poor one makes it through to implementation, the development process has failed.

Objectivity by itself isn't enough, though. Reliable development requires *enthusiastic* objectivity. The cold, hard analysis required for effective development will overwhelm most ideas unless they're supported by genuine enthusiasm. Put another way, if an idea reaches the development stage, the burden of proof is on those who would find it impractical. How do you accomplish this? By ensuring that the idea has a champion to fight for it until it's proved unworkable.

Because they begin with the necessary enthusiasm, it is normally most efficient to have the person or persons who came up with the discovery at least participate in, if not direct, the development. Yes, they will probably be biased, but they will also have the enthusiasm required to take the idea through the hard work of development.

All this makes development sound like a major effort, such as the long months required several years ago to recast U.S. Savings Bonds from a so-so investment instrument into a tremendously attractive one. Some development does require a major effort, but much of it does not. An individual who suggests that changes be made in an interoffice routing slip may take only minutes to come up with the idea and then may develop it ready to implement within an hour. That doesn't make the discovery and the development any less important, and enthusiastic objectivity is still required. Just as everyone needs to be an effective scout, so everyone needs to be an effective designer and critic.

Efficient Implementation

Who in the world would ever associate creativity with implementation? For years, management texts spoke of managers as decision makers, scarcely mentioning implementation. "Implementation isn't management, and it certainly isn't creative." "Implementation is engineering or marketing or somebody else's job; give it to them and let them get it done."

The system never worked well, and it's an almost sure recipe for failure today. With cycle time shrinking in company after company, the time it takes to move from development to production becomes critical. Just hurrying up the process doesn't work; do that and you pay for it later in lost sales, product or service reworking and redesign, and repair or replacement. This makes creativity critical, so you can reduce the time from development to production and still do the job well. And the measure of the efficiency of implementation is the combination of how quickly and how effectively the idea moves from development to production.

This holds true for new practices and processes just as strongly as it does for products and services. A company's internal structure and processes may change as quickly as what it produces; look at the increasing number of ad hoc teams in even the most traditional organizations today. If a company needs a changed practice or process, it probably needs it *yesterday*. And it probably will need a new one tomorrow.

Above all else, the impresarios responsible for implementation must know and understand *both the organization and the individuals in it*. They must know where to get support and where there will be resistance; who can work together effectively; who will contribute willingly and who must be worked around. Above all else, the impresarios must have a sharp feel for the capabilities of the units and individuals involved. Is it safe simply to delegate, or must one delegate but follow up carefully, or retain control and delegate only the carrying out of specific decisions. Technical knowledge is important, of course, but understanding the organizational system and the key people in it is far more important.

Again, what gets implemented varies widely. It may require no more than selling a minor process change to accounting or the MIS department. It may mean convincing top management to institute a very different leadership development program. Or it may entail pulling a team together from several major departments in a high-priority effort to beat a competitor to market with a new service.

So the individual needs not only a deep knowledge of the organization and its people but real *creative interpersonal skills*. If you've never heard that term before, you should have. Because interpersonal relationships are both critical and highly complex, no area needs creativity more than this. Look at a few quick examples:

- Most books and seminars on conflict resolution present it as a series of principles or steps; Fisher and Ury propose three principles, while Weeks offers "eight essential steps." If you think this means that you can follow a "cookbook" approach, you haven't been involved in conflict resolution. It requires not only great expertise but also the constantly creative application of the expertise.

- What do you do when two department heads are at each other's throats and a new service is scheduled to hit the streets in sixty days? If you're very good, you find quick answers to the question of what the payoff is for each of them—then make it strong enough that they're willing to work with each other to get it. Do you imagine, even for a moment, that you can do that without a great deal of creativity?
- Increasingly, implementation involves customers and suppliers. Software companies need customers as beta testers. Apparel manufacturers need customers who will hook them into their point-of-sale systems and suppliers who will accept orders electronically. But many of these relationships have been stressful in the past, and there's always the danger of purloined information. Creativity to the rescue again, or else.

Notice how the creative skills required change from phase to phase. Discovery requires frame flexibility, even frame breaking, by scouts. Development requires the creative combination of enthusiasm for the new product, service, practice, or process (by the designers) and a coldly objective assessment of its benefits and problems (by the critics). Implementation shifts to the interpersonal realm, where creativity directs itself toward anticipating and resolving potential conflict. The more creatively impresarios meet, uncover, and resolve conflict, the more efficiently implementation takes place.

Efficient Production and Improvement

Here I can be short. Masaaki Imai's book *Kaizen: The Key to Japan's Competitive Success* was published in the United States in 1986. Since then, the best companies have known that production and process improvement are inseparable. The problem is that Imai didn't go far enough. The same players who contribute practice and process improvements can as easily suggest product and service improvements in the areas they know. This redeems the routine work that remains in your organization; when performed with a creative, alert mind, it begins to suggest its own improvements. Efficient production becomes inseparable from effective improvement. In short, technicians become learners, and vice versa.

Let me address a final question here. In Chapter 3, I spoke of the necessity for ownership and entrepreneurship in a constantly creative organization. Now we can raise the question only touched on there: When an individual discovers a potentially salable product or service, what should his or her involvement be from that point on?

I've already suggested that the individual who discovers the idea should own the development of it. That seems straightforward; if someone else develops the idea, the individual is both relieved of the hard work of development and of the satisfaction of seeing his or her discovery take form. Much the same argument can be made for implementation, since tremendous learning takes place there also.

The argument lacks the same force when it comes to the production and improvement phase. How much learning is there after the new product or service, practice or process, is implemented? I doubt one can generalize. If someone has come up with an innovative leadership development program, she might well want to operate it for several years. Or she might not. I raise the issue precisely because I don't believe a simple answer exists, but I think you might want to keep the question in mind.

Remember, if creative individuals have a single characteristic in common, it is that they are *individuals*. They don't just value diversity, they create it! You may well alternately rejoice in this fact and curse it. If your organization is constantly creative, however, you will never escape it.

Cycles Within Cycles Between Cycles

Now I must correct a misleading impression I've created through this chapter: that the stages of the innovation cycle are clear and distinct, that discovery is discovery and production is production and never the twains shall meet on the innovation twack. Wrong! All the stages are occurring constantly, both independently and as part of other stages. How can you have improvement if it doesn't begin with the discovery of a problem somewhere? How can a scout even communicate the discovery to the designers and critics if she can't produce a working model—even if the model is a purely mental one? How can critics learn how valid their evaluations were if they don't talk with impresarios and technicians to see what actually happened.

In a constantly creative organization, the wheels are always turning, and within these wheels other wheels are as surely turning. Impresarios talk with designers and critics, and in the dialogue discover a more effective way to implement part of the design. Students talk to these same designers and critics to find out just what one feature of the service accomplishes, and together they discover a better solution, then develop and implement it. The flow gets sloppy and messy and even chaotic at times, as Tom Peters keeps pointing out.[4] Remarkably enough, companies that accept and go with this flow often seem to be the ones that prosper in today's world. Now that's efficiency!

What to Do Now

Read the following suggestions. Find the one that seems most relevant to your organization. How can you begin to apply it right now?

1. If you want a creative but more efficient organization, start searching now for all the elaboration that goes on in your organization. When you find it, you've found an individual or a unit that has boring work or not enough work. Spend some effort there. What can you do to make the jobs more interesting and to link them directly to the goals of the organization? Do it.

2. Use the idea of elaboration in another way. Examine the products or services that you generate. How much time is your organization spending elaborating them, creating changes merely for the sake of change that increase the value of the product or service minimally either for you or your customer? If you're doing

much of this, you're wasting time. Even worse, you're spinning your wheels, handing a golden opportunity to a hungry competitor. Move the operation back one step, so that it's generating true, value-creating improvements. If you can't do this, and perhaps even if you can, make sure that you have enough people who see themselves as scouts. If all you can do is elaborate on your current products or services, it's time for a serious breakthrough.

3. Look closely at the description of efficiency in each phase of the innovation process. Identify where these phases occur in your organization, discuss the nature of efficiency in that phase with the people involved in it, and then see if you can't work out some more exact criteria for efficiency in *your* organization. Get everyone thinking about efficiency, but don't put the cart before the horse. Get them thinking about innovation and their creative contribution to it—and then get them thinking about how they can do this most efficiently.

4. Spend some serious time thinking about ownership and creativity in your organization. When a good new idea comes up, who gets to develop and implement it? Does the originator keep ownership? If not, why not? If yes, for how long? Do you push your scouts to become familiar with the process at least as far as implementation? How do the designers and critics get involved, and what ownership do they have? You need a strategy, one that rewards innovation with ownership, but adapts to the individual creating it.

5. Finally, make it real to everyone that you expect each member of the organization to be a scout and a learner. Many of them will also be designers, critics, and impresarios, but *all* of them should constantly be scouting and learning. *All* of them.

Chapter 7

How to Get and Keep Creative Players

Innovation requires major effort. It requires hard work on the part of performing, capable people—the scarcest resource in any organization.

—Peter Drucker

For a creative organization to operate, it must recruit, develop, retain, motivate, and reward its complement of Drucker's "performing, capable people." If it succeeds at this, it will have far more performing, capable people than conventional organizations its size. It will always need more; such people will still remain a scarce resource for it. The more successful a creative organization becomes, the more possibilities it sees: "Just think what we could do if we only had two more salespeople like. . . ."

I can't give you a solution to the problem; none exists. But I can give you eight keys to recruiting, developing, retaining, motivating, and rewarding a creative work force.

Key 1. Create a System

A creative organization fits all its human resources management practices together into a coherent system that supports the type of organization described in Chapters 1 through 6.

One of the basic problems in changing an organization is that it truly is a system and can't be changed piecemeal. Yet it has to be; trying to change all of an organization overnight closely resembles becoming an overnight celebrity: It usually takes years.

What do you do? You carefully develop a picture of what the organization should be, shape a vision if you will, and then begin to change the organization so that it gets closer and closer to that vision. Motorola provides an excellent example of this. You've heard of its "Six Sigma" quality—fewer than ten defects per million parts. It didn't begin there. Robert Galvin had a clear idea of where he wanted the company to go, but he began with quality goals far more attainable by the organization. Then, as each was met, he raised the ante. Now, in some parts of the corporation, Six Sigma quality is a reality, and the goal has become no defects per million.

Nowhere is a coherent overall vision more important than in your human resources management practices. No organization can succeed just by pasting creative practices onto its existing system. However, you'll need to begin by changing just a few areas, then moving on until more and more of the system is changed. This will generate discomfort and a certain amount of confusion along the way, but if your vision is clear the organization will pass through the problems and emerge as far more creative on the other side.

A final point: Develop a clear vision of your own and ignore the fads! Not that you shouldn't keep up with what's happening in the human resources management area; you, or your VP for HRM, should. Just don't decide to do something because "everyone else is doing it" or because some new guru is promoting it. Remember, less than one-third of those everyone elses will succeed, and most gurus rise and fall with the times. If a new program fits your strategy, use it, by all means. If it doesn't? Forget it, no matter how great it sounds. If a time should come when it really will help, implement it then—when implementing it will probably be both cheaper and safer.

Where do you focus your HRM system? Look at Chapters 1 through 6 again. The job of the HRM system is to support the constantly creative organization described in these chapters. Keys 2 through 8 spell out some of the characteristics such a system must have. Remember, though, the overall system, focused on supporting a constantly creative organization, is what really counts.

Key 2. Hire Creative People

A creative organization hires creative people.

That certainly sounds obvious, and it is. But its execution requires careful planning and constant attention.

Let's look at one of the irritating facts of life. The most creative students are the ones who drop out of college. (I dropped out of my master's business program because instead of making me more creative it was driving me deeper and deeper into a rut.) Both Bill Gates and Michael Dell dropped out of major universities to start computer companies that today generate billions of dollars in revenue. Creative people also drop out of corporations. Thousands of corporate citizens jump at the opportunity for early retirement to start their own businesses, while others simply resign to start theirs.

So, how do you use these facts to your advantage?

• *You develop such a reputation as a creative, exciting organization that the line forms outside your door.* No, I'm not kidding. How do you think Microsoft or Carnegie Mellon's AI unit get such talented people? If you build a constantly creative organization, creative people will know it and they will come.

• *To keep up the talent flow, you encourage your current players to recommend new hires to you.* Various companies at one time or another have used this "bounty" system, and it can work well. It's based on the premise that your effective performers will recommend people like themselves and/or people with whom they would like to work.

• *To reward those who recommend people for your company, you might consider a two-step process.* If the individual recommended is hired, you pay a bonus to the player who recommended her. Then, if that person is still employed and performing well after six months or a year, you pay a second bonus. But you may not have to pay any bonus; if your players are happy enough with the organization, they may consider that they're doing their friends a favor just by recommending you.

• *You'll need to continue recruiting from colleges and universities, but you might want to consider making contact with potential hires in high school, then following the outstanding ones through college before hiring them permanently.* This requires careful planning. You establish working relationships with one or several high schools (depending on your size and theirs). You develop a way to identify their students with high creativity—who may or may not be among their academically best students. Then you offer them after-school and summer jobs. You follow the cream of the crop to college, and perhaps even help them financially.

• *Alternatively, you might want to set up cooperative work-study programs with one or more universities or colleges.* These programs have three important benefits. (1) Because you pay students for the time they work with you, you help less well-to-do individuals make it through college. (2) You get to keep up with the individuals' progress, which makes it easier to make a hire/no hire decision when they graduate. (3) If you provide challenging and creative work to individuals, you may provide the incentive they need to remain in school. (Remember, the most creative tend to drop out.)

The program takes managing, but it creates a true win-win-win situation for you, the schools, and the students. Although I have no figures on this, I suspect that individuals hired through such a program remain much longer with the firm that hired them than those simply hired on the basis of their college record and a few interviews.

One final note. You want creative individuals, but you want creative individuals who are willing to discipline their creativity to the organization's objectives. This makes the work-study alternative particularly effective, because it gives both you and the students the opportunity to discover whether they can commit to your organization's goals.

Key 3. Select for a Lifetime Contribution

A creative organization hires individuals to make a lifetime contribution, not to fill a specific position.

Yes, she may not want to spend a lifetime with your organization. Yes, you may have to cut staff and he may be let go. But you have to begin with the assumption that you're hiring the individual for a ten-, twenty-, or thirty-year contribution. You're hiring a package of motivations, capabilities, and potentials, not just a systems analyst with broad client-server experience. Certainly it's a bonus if he has such experiences, but never at the expense of long-term potential. What if this kind of potential isn't apparent? Hire the individual on a project basis, with the clear understanding that he probably won't become a permanent member of the organization.

Many of the best corporations already take this approach. Hewlett-Packard interviews and interviews and interviews individuals before it makes a hiring decision. So does Mazda, and just for assembly-line positions. Or WordPerfect, for customer-support positions. These companies may look for a specific set of skills, for instance, electrical engineering, math ability, or experience in dealing with the public. But the criteria that really matter to them are personal attributes and abilities that will contribute to the company for years, not just for weeks or months.

If you want a continually creative organization, you certainly can do no less.

Key 4. Integrate Training and Operations

A creative organization trains constantly and integrates the training into its ongoing operations.

From reading the popular press, you might think that training solves a multitude of ills. And it does, but only if the training is related to the present and future activities of the individual being trained. Consistently creative organizations spend a minimum of time on "familiarization" and "overview" training. Even when the training (such as management or leadership development) is designed to develop players, it's built around how work is really performed in the organization.[1]

Any training should begin with orientation or, if you'll pardon the phrase, indoctrination. New members of the organization need to understand its goals, its structure, its culture, and—particularly—how it differs from other organizations they may be familiar with. The training can be provided in a variety of ways. The individual's manager or mentor should play a major part, with this augmented by self-paced training, computer-based training, videos, and formal classroom training. Effective training at the start helps the individual to become effective far sooner than she otherwise would.[2]

Training should be career-long, of course. Because each organization differs from every other, it's very difficult to make general recommendations on what ought to be covered. You do need career and managerial development, of course, though it should include far more than a few training courses. Good mentoring and job rotation programs are at least as important as formal training.

What about creativity training? Creativity training is important, but only when it's integrated with the other aspects of the HRM system. Most important, if you're going to train people to be more creative, you should expect them to apply this new ability the moment they return to the job. Do you remember really innovative training you've tried to apply back on the job, only to find it wasn't wanted? I certainly do. Don't impose this on your performers. Provide creativity training, but first make sure that those who receive it will have the opportunity to apply it when they finish their training.

Key 5. Provide Challenging Work

A creative organization makes the challenge and worth of the work itself the most important motivator for high performance—for everyone.

How often have you seen or heard about the following situation? A company hires talented and creative individuals, promising them the chance to "make a real contribution." Then these individuals endure months or even years of routine and boring jobs as they work their way up the corporate ladder to a job that permits them to be creative. Is it any wonder that so many new college hires leave within two years? And what about those who stay? How much drive and creativity do they have left after they've "paid their dues"? Is it any wonder that so many senior workers and managers are *antichange* agents?

Everyone, clerks included, should be making contributions from the beginning. Is this practical? Yes. Is it easy? No. You should be aware, however, that the military services are extremely adept at doing just this. A lieutenant or captain may have responsibility for a project that his or her counterpart in private industry wouldn't have a shot at for years. Not all private industry is this way, though. Ralph Sarich is CEO of Orbital Engine Company in Perth, Australia, which builds very advanced engines. He lets new people get their feet wet, with a vengeance: "We throw people into deep water fast. We give them the feeling that the company depends on them, and they learn to respect that responsibility."[3]

Then continue the emphasis on challenge for the player's working lifetime. Effective performers should earn well, but don't ever think of pay as the primary motivator. You want everyone, from junior clerk to CEO, to think of his or her job first as a real challenge. W. L. Gore, among many other innovative companies, has explicit company policies *not* to pay unusually high salaries.

Several months ago, after one of my colleagues had just returned from vacation, I asked him if he had enjoyed himself. "It was great," he said, "but, you know, the last few days I was really looking forward to getting back to work." That's how you want each and every one of your players—yourself included—to feel.

Key 6. Balance People and Jobs

Creative organizations are expert at balancing people and work, creative and routine work, and individual and team work.

If your first thought is, how do I set up an organization to do this?, forget it. If you've read and followed what the first six chapters urged, you won't have to do much. If the organization is flexible enough, individuals will find their places. And then they will find new places as their abilities and motivation change.

This will be particularly true if you use teams. Teams need some balancing; you can't staff teams without regard to the abilities and preferences of their members. But once a team is working effectively, it will accomplish much of the balancing function for you. The more self-managing a team becomes, the more highly skilled it will become at balancing tasks and people. Even project teams can perform this function for you, providing that they have the opportunity to work together intensely enough to form a cohesive group.

What, then, do *you* do? You look out for the individuals who don't want to perform on teams, who want to make their contributions individually. They do exist, there are lots of them in fact, and they're talented. They need to find the niches where they can make their individual contributions and not to be forced cookie-cutter-style into teams. You'll find that some of these individuals will decide that they really want to be part of a team. Others will be rampantly individualistic to the end of their careers. So be it; even in our team-oriented world, solitary individuals can still make contributions. Ensure that there is a place where they can contribute effectively. If that place isn't in your organization, help them gently but firmly to find their slot somewhere else.

Key 7. Keep Compensation Congruent With Creativity

A creative organization doesn't motivate by money, but it ensures that its compensation system is congruent with its emphasis on creativity

We looked very briefly at motivation by money. Now we take a slightly closer look at its role in creativity. There are two key points. First, creativity cannot be motivated by money alone. (Nor, for that matter, can quality or even sustained productivity.) Second, money rewards must be consistent with individual and team contributions—or they will act as powerful demotivators. In other words, in a continually creative organization, the compensation system is more apt to cause problems than to solve them. Sorry!

Despite what you may have read, money is not a good primary motivator of performance, and certainly not of creative performance. The challenge of the job and the autonomy and support to do the job well are far more powerful. I've already mentioned W. T. Gore, maker of Goretex, one of the most flexible and creative employers in the United States. The company has a strict policy that it will not recruit by offering higher salaries than its competitors. What it offers instead is the challenge of working there—and it gets plenty of takers.

Then is money unimportant? Not at all. But you must realize how it functions in a creative organization. *Cash McCall* was a movie made years ago about the oil business. In it, the heroine expressed her surprise to the hero that with the millions he already had he still cared about making more money. "You don't understand," he said. "Money's just the way you keep score."

That's how creative performers see it too. You can't get high performance from them with money—but you'd better not give the high salaries to your noncreative players. As with any other aspect of compensation, the money needs to be there for the individuals who contribute to the company's strategic goals. Most performers have a highly developed sense of what's fair. When they commit themselves to the organization's goals and produce for the organization, they expect to be rewarded commensurately for it.

Don't begin with the money; begin with the challenge. Then, when they rise to the challenge, pay them for it. You may pay them as individuals or as teams, or both. You may pay them through higher salaries, through bonuses, or (most probably) through a combination of the two. You can count on spending more time developing and revising an effective compensation schedule than you ever expected to. When it seems to be a burden, just keep in mind: For creative people, money won't motivate, but it certainly will *de*motivate.

Key 8. Focus *All* Incentives on Creativity

A creative organization ensures that all its incentives fit together to support creative performance.

Didn't we just cover incentives when we talked about challenge and money? Yes—and no. Specifically, we talked about the most visible incentives. At best, however, they form only the tip of the proverbial iceberg. These are some of the incentives that lie below the water:

- Who gets promoted, and why
- What will really get you into trouble, especially what might get you fired
- What will get you noticed, positively or negatively
- What will get you more autonomy or a bigger budget, or both
- Even who gets the choice parking spots (Sound silly? If you have reserved parking, just talk with whoever administers it and ask if there's ever controversy when the rules about who gets what change.)

These are the bare bones. Now here are the same bones with some meat on them:

- The organization stresses teamwork and gives special plaques honoring it—but appraises and promotes on the basis of individual performance.
- The organization stresses the importance of frontline performers, but does nothing to prevent customers from berating and threatening them.
- The organization stresses quality and innovation, but gives bonuses based on profitability alone.
- The organization stresses autonomy and initiative, but the key spots go to those who never make waves.

And on, and on, and on.

For obvious reasons, organizations tend to concentrate on their formal compensation plan as a primary motivator. We've already seen that it needs to track, not lead, creativity. But so does everything else. Promotions, bonuses, key jobs, choice assignments—in a creative organization all these dovetail with the formal compensation plan. When the name of the game is teamwork, players who are effective team players get noticed. When innovation is the name of the game, performers who play it safe find themselves at the end of the line for *all* the goodies—including the good parking spaces.

Aligning all the incentives is the organizational equivalent of painting the Golden Gate Bridge: It's never easy, and as soon as you finish it's time to start all over. But it must be done. If your organization is small, the responsibility should belong to you or another top manager. If it's larger, the executive committee or its equivalent should have alignment on its agenda at least once a year. I can't back this with hard research, but my experience suggests that conflicting incentives are responsible for an immense amount of waste in most organizations.

What to Do Now

An HRM system that supports a constantly creative organization must be a *system*, with every part reinforcing the whole. However, the only way you can begin is by identifying the points where your interventions will produce the greatest results. I end this chapter with a list of the eight keys to an HRM system that truly supports a constantly creative organization. Use the same procedure as before, rating your organization from 0 (not true of it at all) to 10 (completely true of it) on each rule. Then connect the ratings.

The Eight Rules for a Creative HRM System

1. Our organization fits all its human resources management practices together into a coherent system that supports constant creativity.   0———5———10

2. We consistently hire creative people.   0———5———10

3. We hire performers primarily to make a lifetime contribution, not just to fill a specific job.   0———5———10

4. We train constantly and integrate the training into our ongoing operations.   0———5———10

5. We make the challenge and worth of the work itself the most important motivator for high performance—for everyone.   0———5———10

6. We are expert at balancing people and work, creative and routine work, and individual and team work.   0———5———10

7. We don't motivate by money, but our compensation system is congruent with our emphasis on creativity.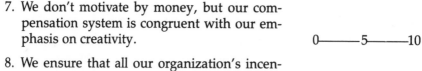

8. We ensure that all our organization's incentives fit together to support creative performance.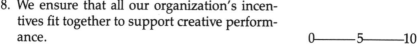

You've created another visual profile of your current organization, this one focused on what you need to do to support creativity by means of your human resources management system. After you've looked over the following eight suggestions, keyed to the rules for a creative HRM system, choose one or two suggestions to implement now. Then build on them.

1. *Does your organization not fit all its human resource management practices together into a coherent system that supports constant creativity?* The odds are good that it doesn't; HRM practices don't systematically support creativity in most organizations. Don't let that deter you from beginning now to create such a system. Look at your basic HRM processes: recruiting, training, compensating, and promoting. Ask two questions of each specific system or subsystem. First, to what extent does it support creativity? Second, what does it really support? Do this honestly and you'll have an excellent idea of the work you need to do to become constantly creative.

At the same time, you should initiate a dialogue with your HR Manager and her department. Start spelling out your goals for a new HRM system. Your HR folks may not be enthusiastic about it; if that's the case, listen carefully and understand why. On the other hand, they may jump at the chance to make the change; if so, make sure they don't get too far ahead of the rest of the organization.

2. *Do you fail to consistently hire creative people?* This chapter contains some specific suggestions on this point. Start by building a relationship with a high school or community college. You have summer, part-time, and cooperative work-study jobs to offer, as well as the opportunity for permanent employment down the road. Most schools find that very attractive. Find one that does,

solicit its help in identifying the kind of creative performer you're looking for, then go on from there.

3. *Do you hire performers primarily to fill a specific job rather than to make a lifetime contribution?* Changing this practice may sound simple; let me assure you it isn't. Hiring for specific jobs is a way of life in most companies. Even when a trainee is hired, HR usually has in mind a specific job a few pay grades higher. If your organization is large, you probably have very specific qualification standards for many of the jobs. Select a few key jobs, but not your top ones. Negotiate with the HRM department if you have to, so you're not bound by tight specific qualifications. Then you and several other managers (if available) interview the candidates, concentrating on their potential to contribute to the organization over a five- to fifteen-year period. Select the ones with the greatest potential, and make it clear to the individuals why they were selected. Then keep close watch, both to see how they develop *and* to make sure that the organization doesn't simply typecast them in their current positions. After you've done this several times, you may find that it becomes addictive.

4. *Do you fail to train constantly and integrate the training into your ongoing operations?* This fits closely with hiring individuals for their potential lifetime contribution. These individuals must be trained for their current positions but also developed into the type of performer who can make the long-term contribution you want. Let me suggest a very simple start. Hold a regular review of the training your people get with your team leaders, direct reports, and/or any other managers in the organization. Look at the relevance of the training in general, but look for one point in particular: How often did the individual get to apply her training *immediately after* she received it? No fudging, now; be cruelly honest with this one. You can make the single greatest improvement in your training program by insisting that, to the maximum extent possible, individuals receive training only when they can use it immediately upon returning to the job.

5. *Do you make something other than the challenge and worth of the work itself the most important motivator(s) for high performance?* Have you been trying to motivate high performance, or even creative performance, with dollars? Or simply by telling players

that you want them to be creative? Or by motivational speeches, posters, and creativity training? Has the approach lived up to your hopes? Probably not. Performers become creative when they are committed to challenging tasks that they can accomplish. If your company hasn't organized work so that it's challenging, the time to change has come. Find an experienced internal or external consultant, then start small and keep building.

6. *Are you poor at balancing people and work, creative and routine work, and individual and team work?* Every company has to find this balance, and the balance is different with each company. Begin by developing challenging work that calls for creativity. As performers begin to do this work, you'll see the need for balance develop (as when creative teams get bogged down by routine work). You won't have to do all the balancing; as your organization develops, you'll have to do less and less of it. But you do need to see that it gets done. Be especially mindful of situations in which individuals don't fit their assigned duties or confirmed individualists are being forced to work as part of teams. You won't get creativity in either situation, so the faster you can spot them and change them, the better.

7. *Do you try to motivate primarily by money? Is your compensation system at odds with your emphasis on creativity?* Companies that don't rely on challenging work to motivate performers usually rely on money. Even when they do value creativity, the compensation system often rewards safe, trouble-free players or those with a direct relationship to profit production more than it does its most creative performers. If what you want is creativity, make sure that it's what is rewarded. Money isn't everything, but, as they say, it talks—and you want your creative individuals to hear the right message.

8. *Do all your organization's incentives not fit together to support creativity?* You can make more progress if you look at all your organization's incentives, not just pay. After looking at compensation, expand your view and look at *everything* that your firm gives as perks. Look at stock options, bonuses, parking places, time off, formal and informal recognition, promotion, anything players value that your company controls. (I'd exempt formal benefits, like health and life insurance and basic retirement plans,

but not too much else.) Begin with those that are easiest to change and modify them to support creativity. Then continue the process. It will take a while—months, possibly even years—but if you pursue it systematically you'll begin to reap significant performance rewards. And it won't necessarily cost you a single cent more than you're paying now; you'll just be using incentives in a far more targeted manner.

Chapter 8

How Teams Promote Creativity

A camel is a horse designed by a committee. A giraffe is a horse designed by a team of people who didn't want to be on the team but were put there by a manager who didn't really believe in teams but whose organization had just made a "strategic commitment" to teams.

—Anonymous

Does your organization use self-managing teams? Is it attempting to become a learning organization? Did it try one or more of these tactics and only partly succeed? If your answer to any of these questions is yes, you may find the next two chapters interesting. My thesis is simple: The bottom line of teams and learning organizations is that they help produce and then help support constantly creative organizations. If you look at them from this point of view, and if you've decided to develop a creative organization, you may find new life in one or both of these ways of operating.

Suppose you decide to take an Alaskan cruise. Boarding the ship in Vancouver, you remain below deck for the seven days of the cruise. You see excellent scenery through your porthole, eat good food, and meet some new and interesting people. All well and good. But is it complete?

Of course not. Why go on a cruise unless you're going to spend time on deck, see the glaciers and wildlife, visit the scenic areas, walk about and talk with the people you meet. Until you do this, you miss the real payoff from the cruise—and that's exactly what happens when you implement self-managing teams or try to develop a learning organization without seeing creativity as the core of the process. Used as a means to liberate the creativity of your organization, each is powerful—and the two combined are more powerful. Without the creativity, neither will reach their potential. This and the following chapter briefly explain why.

Why Use Teams?

Why are teams so popular these days, so popular in fact that many writers identify them as *the* way to manage an organization?[1] One answer: They're a fad, promising higher quality and quantity and lower cycle time to companies starving for all three. Teams have worked extremely well for a small number of companies; we have no idea yet how well they deliver on a broad scale. We do know, however, where their strengths lie.

First, and overwhelmingly so, *teams work when they successfully combine within a single team a set of functions or skills that were previously located in different organizations.* The first successful self-directing work teams, in Procter & Gamble's Paper Products Division and at the Topeka (Kansas) Gaines Dog Food Plant, combined blue-collar skills. The Saturn plant in Spring Hill, Tennessee, a much more recent creation, does the same thing. Teams at a wide variety of insurance and financial organizations accomplish the same goal for clerical work. And the Chrysler Corporation's success in using multifunctional teams to bring new cars to market in record time and within budget illustrates the value of multifunctional teams composed of highly skilled positions.

Effective teams can combine *four* different types of previously separated work:

1. They can combine different *skills* that were previously located in several different functions. Thus Chrysler's teams combine design, manufacturing, marketing, and a host of other skills. Because each function has its own language, its own point of view, its own priorities—in other words, its own "culture"—

combining them on a team permits each one to develop and use a broader perspective. They can focus more easily on the mission instead of on their more limited functional concerns.

2. They can combine *tasks* from several organizations and thus a sequential work flow into a simultaneous one. When successful, this dramatically reduces the time needed to accomplish the overall task. Chrysler's use of teams and Ford's earlier Team Taurus exemplify this; so do the hundreds of clerical operations in which teams have reduced time and increased productivity.[2]

Note that combining skills or functions and combining tasks are related but not identical tactics. When a process is performed by individuals with different skills or from different functions, the problems are caused by their different languages, points of view, and priorities. When a process spans several different organizations, the organizational boundaries themselves are the problem. Although different organizations often mean different functions or skills, neither can be reduced completely to the other.

3. They can include *support functions* that were previously performed outside the team. For example, teams often do their own budgeting and planning and may be responsible for obtaining and maintaining their supplies and materials.

4. Finally, they can perform many of the *duties previously performed by supervisors*. They often do their own hiring, determine individual appraisals and pay, and may even participate in selecting the next-higher-level "manager."

Combining these functions in one relatively small team sharply reduces the lines of communication, waiting times, conflicting priorities, and attempts to fix blame on "them" typically found in a conventional organization. When they internalize the supervisory function, they become self-managing and begin to realize their full potential. You may find the next two advantages of teams in a variety of teams, but they will always be most obvious in self-managing teams.

Second, *when teams are self-managing they allow individuals to exercise significantly more control over their work processes*. This autonomy allows not only teams but individuals to gain more control over their own success. Because effective teams are flexible, individual members can be used in ways that capitalize on their strengths, rather than simply within the confines of a narrow job. When teams perform a variety of relatively low-skilled tasks, individuals have the opportunity to learn and to perform a variety of tasks. Even when the tasks involved are highly skilled, such as those of engineers, individuals can learn to tailor their contributions in ways that will best integrate with the work of others.[3]

Third, *self-managing teams increase individual commitment to the job and the organization's goals.* Because work as part of an effective team is challenging and rewarding for its own sake, and because individuals have more control over their critical success factors, they invest more of themselves in their jobs. The work, together with the social benefits of serving on a cohesive team, becomes a powerful motivator in its own right.

Teams contribute other benefits to organizations, but these three are by far the most important. And they are the basic link between the use of self-managing teams and constant creativity in the organization. Before we look at how creative organizations can use teams, however, we need to take a quick look at the characteristics that teams require for success.

When (and When Not) to Use Teams

Teams *may* produce these benefits, but nothing guarantees that they will. Like most organizational forms, teams flourish in certain circumstances and fail in others. All organizations, but particularly creative organizations, need to understand when teams will be successful and when they will not be.

So, how do you tell the difference? Successful teams have nine characteristics that contribute directly to their success. Any team should have these characteristics; self-managing teams *must* have them. The lack of even one of the characteristics will be damaging and perhaps even fatal. Here they are, modified slightly from my book *Teampower:*[4]

1. *The individual creating the team and the team members have shared values that support teamwork.* If not, the team will never get off the ground. If higher levels in the organization don't share these values, the team may succeed at first but its future will be in doubt.
2. *The team has clear, worthwhile, compelling goals. Clear*, so that each team member knows what should be done. *Worthwhile*, so that they seem worth committing to. *Compelling*, so that the team is not steamrolled by other, more pressing goals.
3. *These goals can be accomplished only by a team.* When the work can be done by an individual, a team will cost more and be less effective.
4. *There is a genuine need for each member of the team.* "Jane doesn't have enough to do" or "Let's put Charlie on the team—maybe he'll learn something" are killer ways to staff a team. Teams deal with internal problems far more quickly when they need everyone on the team in order to succeed.
5. *Each member of the team is committed to the team goals.* Want to kill a team quickly? Just let the critical part of each member's performance appraisal be done by a supervisor who has no interest in the success of the team. Or who wants an outcome favorable to her function, no matter what.
6. *The team has specific, measurable objectives to accomplish as a team.* Without these objectives, the team typically wallows or becomes dominated by the agenda of one or two individuals.
7. *The team gets effective feedback on its performance.* Effective feedback is accurate, specific, prompt, direct, reliable, and appropriate. Without it, the team has no way of telling if it is achieving its objectives—and will probably give far too much weight to internal, rather than goal-directed, criteria.
8. *There are specific rewards for team performance, not just individual performance.* Team performance must *matter*, enough for the team as a whole to be rewarded. If managers back in the individual performers' functions control the rewards, this can kill the group's cohesiveness.

9. *Team members are competent both as individuals and as a team.* They must be highly skilled at working together *and* at their individual specialties. Team skills can be developed through various "team-building" training, but no amount of team skills will ever substitute for the specific competence that the team needs from the individual.

No simple list, this one included, ever guarantees success (or failure). However, if you use teams, or are considering using them, the list will help you make intelligent decisions about them and thus increase the probability that they will be successful.

How to Use Teams Creatively

Look again at the discussion of the three basic strengths of teams. Teams work because they combine necessary functions or skills within the team; because, especially if they are self-managing, they give individuals significantly more control over their work; and because, again especially if they are self-managing, they increase individual commitment to the job and the organization's goals. Think about these strengths in the context of the previous chapters and see what they suggest. Creative organizations require frame flexibility—and how better to start preventing frame-lock than working day after day on a team that combines the different viewpoints of different functions? Creativity requires players who have great autonomy—and teams provide just that. Creativity requires the hard work and risk taking that only the fully committed can support—and teams encourage just this commitment.

Teams also support other characteristics I have discussed; for instance, effective teams are always marked by a high level of trust. The fact that teams support the factors that promote creativity isn't enough, though. Truly effective creative organizations go beyond using teams to promote creativity; they use teams as a positive force in *generating* creativity.

Truly effective teams can show you the way. Once teams become cohesive and begin to stretch their wings, they look for new horizons. Few of them content themselves with doing what they did yesterday; at the least, they want to do it a little better. That's a beginning, but not sufficient for an organization that wants to be (or has become) constantly creative. You want teams to attack new goals and tasks, explore new processes, keep challenging themselves in any way they can. The job is to channel all this energy into products, services, practices, and processes that are new, relevant to the company's strategy, and loaded with value for the company, its customers, and its stakeholders.

How do you accomplish this? By seeing that *every team pursues goals that demand creativity for success*. Masaru Ibuka, the founder of what is now the Sony Corporation, got technical breakthrough after technical breakthrough from his engineers by setting "impossible" targets that they somehow managed to meet. Robert Galvin set impossible target after impossible target for Motorola quality—and the company met them. Creativity is called forth when there are demanding, serious, mind-stretching challenges. Effective teams of all kinds require clear, challenging, worthwhile goals; creative teams require them in spades.

A manager who wants creative teams begins here, but then does much more. Look again at the seven core qualities of a creative organization in Chapter 1. If you intend for teams to be the core of your organization's creativity, each team needs to have every one of those qualities.

What to Do Now

Use the following list as you have the previous ones; rate your organization by putting an X on each scale and then join them with a line.

The Nine Characteristics of Successful Teams

1. Our organization (especially the managers responsible for implementing teams) and the team members have shared values that support teamwork.   0———5———10

2. Our teams have clear, worthwhile, compelling goals.   0———5———10

3. These goals can be accomplished only by a
   team.   0————5————10

4. There is a genuine need for every member of
   each team.   0————5————10

5. All members of the teams are committed to
   the goals of their teams.   0————5————10

6. Each team has specific, measurable objectives
   to accomplish as a team.   0————5————10

7. Each team gets effective feedback on its performance.   0————5————10

8. We have specific rewards for team perform-
   ance, not just individual performance.   0————5————10

9. Members of the teams are competent both as
   individuals and as a team.   0————5————10

No suggestions follow this chart. I included it primarily to help you evaluate the potential for team success in your organization. If the line that connects your answers snakes down the right-hand side, you either have successful teams already or are a prime candidate for instituting them. If it isn't noticeably toward the right-hand side of the page, you have work to do before committing yourself to teams. Many books will help you to prepare your organization for teams. Unless you have strong prior experience with teams, however, I recommend that you also find an experienced consultant to help you implement them.

Chapter 9

Why a Learning Organization Must Be a Creative Organization

"It's appraisal time and I want to give you some feedback" is to real feedback what "Of course I'll still love you in the morning" is to true love.

—Clay Carr

A creative organization must be a learning organization. A learning organization must be a creative organization. Why? Because an organization learns best when it attempts to create a new product, service, practice, or process and then assesses and assimilates the results. Then, by continuing to do this in just the right way, it truly becomes Senge's learning organization, one "that is continually expanding its capacity to create its future."

Are you thinking that this will be a "pie in the sky" chapter, full of impressive words and concepts but short on practicalities. Quite the reverse; this will be one of the most useful chapters in the book. Look back at the systems model introduced in Chapter 2. There I suggested that a creative organizational system needs two forms of feedback, tactical and strategic, for success. Now we return to this theme and explore how to use feedback to develop a learning organization that is a creative system that is a learning system that is a creative organization . . . and so on.

Organizations at all levels require tactical feedback, the "How're we doing?" and "Are we doing things right?" sort of feedback, to stay in business in the short term and to control their futures in the longer term. From this feedback, they determine whether they're achieving their goals, and if they're not, make appropriate adjustments to see that they will. But they need to accompany this with strategic feedback, which asks, "What do you need from us that we're not giving you now?" "Are we doing the right thing?" and "What do you think you'll need five, ten, or twenty years from now?" When organizations get and use this feedback, they can make the basic decisions about what their goals should be five, ten, or even twenty years into the future— and thus begin to create their futures. Let's look in detail at both forms of feedback.

Tactical Feedback, the Feedback That Keeps Us in Business

In my experience, people (including management "authorities") misuse the term *feedback* more often than they get it right. Witness the manager who sits an employee down, leans forward, and states: "I'm going to give you some feedback about your perform-ance, and I expect you to listen carefully!" Or the management writer who advises a supervisor, "Be sure that during the annual appraisal you give the employee useful feedback, not just the rating itself." In the first case, the "feedback" the manager intends to render is most likely his judgment on the employee's performance. In the second, the "feedback" will most likely turn out to be the supervisor's justification for the rating he gives the employee. Neither remotely qualifies as real feedback.

To understand feedback, let's begin with Figure 9-1, a copy of the systems model (Figure 2-6) first presented in Chapter 2. Remember, a system exists to transform decisions about customer requirements into the results desired by the customer. Feedback is always about the relationship between the results and the initial requirements. (From this point on, I use the word *requirements* to mean "goals, objectives and/or requirements" unless I specifically state otherwise. Summarizing them simply as requirements saves

Figure 9-1. The revised systems model.

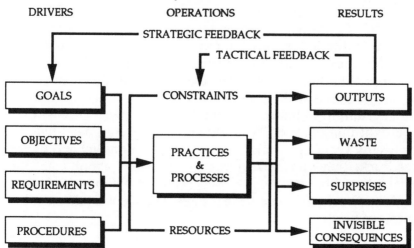

some awkwardness and simplifies the presentation.) But requirements and results aren't enough by themselves. They require a standard, explicit or implicit, by which to evaluate the results. Tactical feedback typically deals with requirements and standards that are relatively specific, even though the standards may not be written down. Here are some examples:

- "Marilyn, the standard you and I agreed on last month says that you'll make at least fifteen cold calls a week, but you've made fewer than ten each week since then. We need to talk about this, so we both understand what's going on."
- "Pierre, six months ago your section committed itself to at least two major new product designs a month. For the last three months, though, you've produced almost twice that many. That's great, and I think it would be really helpful for us to talk about how you're doing it."
- "Tom, you know that the job of everyone here is to delight customers, and that part of the job requires skillful probing to find out how customers really feel. I'd like to go over your conversation with Melanie Vasquez yesterday to help

you understand how you might have used questions more effectively."

Each example illustrates valid feedback. The performer in each case has a standard and knows what kind of performance it requires. The first two standards are very specific. In the third example, Tom and his manager may have very different ideas of what "skillful probing" means—so one result of their conversation might be a better shared understanding of the standard.

What Feedback Is

Given, then, that we have a goal, a standard for telling when it is met, and information about the results of our attempt to meet it, we have a true tactical feedback situation. Now we can use this to define feedback in general:

> Feedback is information that enables an individual, team, or enterprise to evaluate success in achieving a goal against some standard and that can be used to change the goals, the standard, or current performance in ways that make performance more effective.

First, *effective feedback is information, not a judgment.* If I tell you, "That idea of yours just won't cut it," I've given you no feedback at all. I've simply told you my judgment, which in that form will help you little, if at all. If I go on to say, "And here's why it won't cut it," I may be of some help to you.

Second, *effective feedback always compares results with goals (or objectives).* If I don't know your goals, or if mine are different from yours, I may be able to help you in other ways, but I won't be able to give you any really useful feedback. If I say to you, "You'll never get promoted if you keep doing that," and you're not currently interested in a promotion, I haven't given you any feedback. If I go on to say, "And this is why you ought to be worrying about getting a promotion," I may start helping you.

Third, *effective feedback is always based on an explicit or implicit standard*. Because standards are difficult to develop for many jobs, they often remain implicit. For instance, virtually every manager has an implicit standard for her job that says: Never let anyone blindside your boss. Most jobs, in fact, are webs of explicit and implicit standards. Whether formal or informal, these standards determine how useful any supposed feedback will be. If I think my primary job is to produce high-quality studies, but you keep telling me that I don't do enough of them, no real feedback occurs.

Fourth, *effective feedback may change not only performance but standards and goals as well*. Most often, feedback is information that lets performers measure results against standards and change their performance as necessary to better achieve the goals. But feedback may show that the standards are too loose or too tight or even that the goal needs modifying, particularly if it shows that the goal has been met and the time has come to set another goal. Tactical feedback systems, both formal and informal, focus tightly on meeting the goal, but should allow both the standard and the goal to be questioned if the system provides information that supports this questioning. Strategic feedback systems, by contrast, should explicitly question standards and goals.

Fifth, *the purpose of feedback is action, not thought*. After you've given me information, I may know more, but if I can't use it to change what I do, it wasn't feedback.

What Effective Feedback Requires

This leads to the next logical question: What characteristics must feedback have to enable performers and organizations to change what they do? The answer: It must be accurate, specific, prompt, direct, reliable, and appropriate. Let's look at these characteristics in a bit more detail:

1. Effective feedback is *accurate*: It's not simply a guess, someone's opinion, or an estimate of what probably happened.
2. Effective feedback is *specific*: It provides information on

what this performer or group of performers did, not on what some larger group accomplished.

3. Effective feedback is *prompt*: When performers receive it, they have time to change their performance in useful ways.
4. Effective feedback is *direct*: It goes to the performers themselves, not to a staff department or a higher level of management that may both delay and color the feedback as they pass it on.
5. Effective feedback is *reliable*: Performers can count on when they will get it, can rely on its being complete, and know (if it is a report) that the format will not vary from time to time.
6. Effective feedback is *appropriate*: It is in the language of the performers who must use it, and doesn't bury the information they need on three different pages of a 96-page report.[1]

The six characteristics describe feedback within the organization, but they also describe the tactical feedback that the organization as a whole must get from its customers, suppliers, members, stockholders, and other stakeholders on how well it is meeting its goals. Any organization should routinely assess its systems for getting this information to see how reliably they're working—and then make the necessary changes.

Tactical Feedback in a Creative Organization

If any effective organization needs feedback, a creative organization does, and it needs to institutionalize it at every level.

For instance, it needs a feedback system, with all of the six characteristics, that responds to new ideas. Anyone who contributes an idea for a new product, service, practice, or process should be able to count on effective feedback about the idea that is accurate, specific, prompt, direct, reliable, and appropriate. Just saying this isn't enough. In a truly creative environment, the individual with the idea actively solicits the feedback and accepts it without defensiveness. The individuals providing the feedback do so objectively, critiquing the idea, not the contributor. And all parties realize that while the contributor is obligated to listen carefully to the feedback, he or she may not agree with it. The feedback also needs something added to it; whether the idea is promising or not, the individual should get *encouragement* with the feedback.

In these circumstances, feedback evolves into part of an intensive and constant *dialogue* whose goal is finding and evaluating the greatest worth of every idea. The dialogue may be spirited, enthusiastic, heated, even explosive, but it works because it is grounded in a deep commitment to giving and receiving objective feedback.

A creative organization needs this feedback and the dialogue it produces in every nook and cranny, in every function, and at every stage of innovation from discovery through production and improvement. The ten basic attributes described in Chapter 3 are the basis for this dialogue, just as they require the dialogue in order to function effectively. A high level of trust makes dialogue possible, just as dialogue enhances trust. Dialogue forms the core of "telling it like it is," and the basic purpose of telling it like it is is to provide feedback and keep dialogue going. Everyone communicates with everyone else to ensure that the system is alive with dialogue, just as dialogue is a critical part of the communication. And on and on through the rest of the ten attributes (yes, even having fun helps support the dialogical process).

How important is this? In a true dialogue, frames stay flexible, expand, change—and this happens with a minimum of trauma. Dialogue, rooted in objectively given and openly received feedback, also forms the core of the organization's ability to deal with conflict. Nor should anything confine dialogue to the innards of the organization; dialogue with suppliers and customers is just as necessary and just as productive. In short, dialogue promotes, even generates, creative responses in every relationship. And effective feedback is at the core of dialogue.

Strategic Feedback

One of the purposes of feedback is to develop information that can be used to change goals or standards as well as individual or organizational performance. Strategic feedback concentrates on the goals and, secondarily, on the standards. When it is successful, it produces information that helps an organization decide the right thing to do, not how to do it right.

How does an organization, particularly a creative organization, design a feedback system to get and use this information? The answer is at once very simple and very difficult:

> The quality of all feedback, and particularly strategic feedback, depends on (1) the questions it is designed to answer and (2) the openness with which it is received.

We often overlook this basic fact. A thermostat is a simple feedback device. It can be simple because it is designed to respond to a simple question: Does the heat (or air conditioning) need to be turned on or off? Many manufacturing feedback systems that provide information on productivity can be equally simple because they answer the one question: How many? A far more complex feedback system is required to answer the question: How high is our quality, as the customer sees it?

These are all tactical feedback systems, answering the question: How are we doing? Strategic feedback systems, however, answer a different question: What ought we to be doing next month, next year, in ten years? Who should our customers be, and what should we provide them? Should we move toward outsourcing and widespread partnerships or perform all our key functions ourselves?

You don't have to hire a rocket scientist to determine that these are *difficult* questions to answer. Nevertheless, they must be answered, and only strategic feedback can answer them. Just as important, the organization must be willing to listen to the answers it gets and then act on them. But how do you create feedback systems at this level that produce the right answers and bring them to the right people?

First, remember that feedback is useful information that compares results with goals using some standard. To create strategic feedback systems, an organization must begin with its strategic goals. If your basic strategic goal is to be Number 1 or Number 2 in your market (like General Electric), you will create one kind of strategic feedback system. If your goal is to be a successful low-cost producer (like Emerson or Sanyo), your strategic feedback will look very different. And so on through the wide variety of strategic goals that organizations set for themselves. In its simplest terms, you can only get answers to the questions you ask.

Strategic Feedback in a Creative Organization

A traditional organization operating in a settled market can ask relatively simple strategic questions and use relatively rudimentary feedback systems such as conventional customer surveys, golf games with other CEOs, or formal market reseach. But if you've read this far, you almost certainly aren't in that kind of company. And if you intend to have a creative organization, you may use all of these, but you certainly can't settle for them alone. You ask questions like "Where will the market be in five years?" "Where will new customers come from? "How can we hang on to our existing customer base?" "Do we want a different customer base?" To answer these questions, you need a much wider variety of feedback systems, including:

- Constant partnering with your customers and suppliers in order to understand the factors affecting their present and future success through their eyes
- Particularly close relationships with your most progressive customers, to understand and prepare for where they'll be in the next few months and years
- Carefully structured information about your competitors and the government levels that influence you so that you can identify important trends
- An open flow of information within your organization that feeds the experiences of purchasing agents, salespeople, customer service people, repair people, and all others who deal directly with customers upward to the very top levels of the organization

The systems, of course, are only half the answer. The other half is organizational leadership that continually asks the questions and listens openly to the answers, and this requires both frame flexibility and the ability to use conflict to enhance this flexibility. This means, of course, that the more the organization operates as a creative system, the more feedback it can accept and use—and the greater will be its power to create its own future. Remember another basic attribute of creative organizations from Chapter 3: They're always scanning the horizon and proactively anticipating change. Strategic feedback constitutes the core of this process; strategic feedback systems are the way that it's done.

Companies as a whole need strategic feedback systems, but every unit of the organization requires its own strategic feedback system. Every unit has customers and suppliers, and must design its own strategic feedback system to anticipate their needs, requirements, and challenges. Again, units of constantly creative organizations must have highly effective systems because their customers and suppliers are changing so rapidly. Remember that effective creativity is always directed at the organization's goals; each unit in a creative organization stays abreast of both the strategic goals of the total organization and the goals, objectives, and requirements of its immediate customers. No organization can remain creative if even one of its critical units is constantly trying to play catch-up.

What to Do Now

There's no chart here on which to rate your organization. Instead, I want to make two suggestions. It only takes two; if you attempt to implement them, you'll find quite enough to do for now.

First, pick any operation in your organization and examine the feedback it gets—both to the operation itself and to individuals within it. Who gets the feedback? Is the feedback based on shared goals and at least implicit standards? Is it accurate, specific, prompt, direct, reliable, and appropriate? Is the feedback used to improve performance, or is it simply filed away somewhere? Unless all your answers are yes, you will improve both the performance of the operation and the ability of its performers to manage themselves if you help them develop an effective feedback system, based on shared goals and standards. Don't think, "Oh, no, not another automated system!" Although computer system support is important, you may find that a perfectly fine feedback system can be created and maintained without a computer anywhere in sight.

Second, look at the organization as a whole and ask yourself what systems are in place to get and use strategic feedback. Are you even asking the question: How will we need to change to succeed five years from now? If you are asking the question, do you know how to get feedback from your salespeople, your customers, your suppliers, and even your competitors to help you answer that question? And how do you systematically use the feedback you get?

As I said, answering these two questions should keep you gainfully employed for a while.

Chapter 10

How Do You Manage a Constantly Creative Organization?

You don't.

An empowered, creative organization can be led. It cannot be managed.

What a creative organization requires differs so radically from our traditional understanding of management that we're better off not trying to stretch the word to include it. In today's vocabulary, we can only speak of *leading* a creative organization. Leadership is a terminally trendy field right now; I suspect that more books have been written on being a leader since 1980 than in the entire prior history of the Western world. Don't let all the spotlights, banners, and bands fool you, though. The distinction between managing and leading matters—and this is it:

> A *manager* achieves goals by controlling the behavior of workers to achieve them. A *leader* creates a mission and then aligns the efforts of the organization behind this mission.

Let's look at the implications of this distinction.

The Timely Demise of PODC

Almost any manager who came of age in the sixties and beyond learned the Plan → Organize → Direct → Control (PODC) model of management functions. Managers were taught to plan what to accomplish, organize to carry out the plan, direct workers to take the actions necessary to achieve the plan, and then control operations to see that they accomplished the plan. This model closely fitted the hierarchical organization of American corporations over the past century.

The traditional, hierarchical model promoted efficiency, strong internal standards, control of people and information, isolation from the environment, and stability to the point of rigidity. In a stable environment, with stable demand and no discontinuities, it worked. As the competitive environment became progressively less stable during the seventies and eighties, however, management theorists who believed in the model began to tinker with it to make it fit what was happening. All they accomplished was to paste first this and then that new trend onto the same basic framework, in the process destroying much of the usefulness that the framework once had. But no amount of tweaking or modification can make this model work effectively in a changing environment that demands constant creativity. The model is too conceptual, too linear, too much top down, and too much inwardly focused. We need another, dramatically different model.[1]

The Creative Leader Model

Instead of the traditional approach, suppose we took the material in the first nine chapters of this book, sifted it carefully, and tried to distill from it a new idea of what a creative leader does. If we did just this, we'd end up with a model of creative leadership that looks like Figure 10-1.

The model suggests that a leader in a creative organization has six basic functions, which can be grouped into three closely related pairs:

Figure 10-1. The structure of creative leadership.

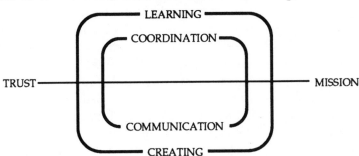

1. Defining the organization's *mission* and aligning the organization with it, while developing and maintaining a high level of *trust* throughout the organization
2. *Coordinating* the organization's activities to achieve its mission and accomplishing this by ensuring that constant *communicating* occurs throughout the organization
3. Developing and maintaining an organization that is continually *learning* because it is constantly *creating* new practices, processes, products, and services of value to itself and its customers.

Let's look very briefly at each pair.

Defining and Aligning With the Mission and Creating Trust

These two functions can be performed *only* by the leader himself. Here's a quick analogy. How would you feel on a flight if you heard the pilot ask the senior flight attendant to take over the plane for a while so he could do something else? Giving someone else basic responsibility for defining the mission, aligning the organization with it, and creating the trust required to accomplish it means turning the piloting of the organization over to someone else.

Does this mean that you do it all yourself? Never—if for no other reason than that you don't have the time. But you lead it and you retain personal responsibility for it. While a leader may involve the entire organization in strategic planning and in implementing the plan, only he can draw everyone's efforts together behind a coherent mission. This has always been the key executive function, even though it was often ignored until recently.

This section may have sounded a little ambiguous to this point. It speaks about two functions, but it refers to defining the mission and aligning the organization with the mission and creating trust—which sounds like three functions. True, it does, but only because we have created an arbitrary distinction between defining a mission and them implementing it in the organization. When leaders attempt to define a mission in isolation from the practical work of aligning the organization with it, it often produces painful effects on market share, stock price, and player loyalty. Creating the mission and then aligning the company with it makes up a single process, and someone who wants to develop and lead a creative organization must become a master of the complete process.

Have you missed the word *values* in this chapter so far? Appropriately so. Those who lead an empowered, creative organization see to it that it develops and lives by a solid core of values. Apple Computer comes to mind again here, with its basic commitment to making computers easier for human beings to use. Values are critical, but they cannot be separated from the organization's mission. I haven't stressed them because senior managers so often treat creating a statement of corporate values as an end in itself. Phooey! If all you do is write a beautiful values statement and ship it out to everyone, the entire effort won't be worth the difference between fifty cents and the cost of a cup of coffee in a good restaurant.

Conversely, when values are integrated with a carefully crafted mission, they become the means for aligning the organization with that mission. We've seen that creative organizations need shared values to support and enhance self-management because committed, self-managed players make an organization creative. Only the leader can ensure that these values come into being and then permeate the organization.

Where does the mission come from? Creative organizations are always scanning the horizon and proactively anticipating change—and leaders are the point people for this effort. Leaders must see that their organizations understand their environment and respond creatively to changes in it. Unifying these changes, however, must be a central mission that remains consistent (though not necessarily identical) through the changes. The role of the mission is to produce this stability and to free the organization to deal with constant change without falling into chaos. And when an organization develops a clear mission, it permits its members to focus on problems and opportunities related to the mission, not on personalities and power structures.

As soon as a leader talks mission and alignment, she must talk trust—and then walk this talk. *An untrusting creative organization* is truly an oxymoron. It literally cannot exist. Please note, though, that the leader's function is not just to develop trust in herself but also to constantly increase the level of trust *throughout* the organization. Only this widespread trust can enable an empowered and creative organization.

An organization characterized by widespread trust commits itself always to look for solutions, not scapegoats. By developing trust and then focusing on the mission, a leader encourages individuals to take sensible risks and sometimes fail. When trust is widely diffused through the organization, individuals are neither shot for failing nor relieved of the responsibility for learning from their mistakes. Put slightly differently, high trust enables the organization to insist on high-level performance and at the same time to treat its players as valuable human beings.

Coordinating and Communicating in Support of the Mission

These two functions can be delegated, and in a fully functioning organization they should be. However, the leader can never simply assume that they are happening.

In an empowered, creative organization, coordinating goes on at every level. If the organization uses fully self-managing teams, these teams do most of the lateral coordinating. Where teams aren't completely self-supporting, they often select the individual(s) who will do the coordinating for them. But whether there are teams or not, coordinating occurs—and it occurs at the lowest possible level.

What makes this kind of organization different from a traditional, hierarchical organization? In a traditional organization, coordinating occurs at the level above the activities that need to be coordinated. If two units—up to and including divisions—disagree, the manager they report to settles the dispute. If the two units belong to very different parent organizations, their disagreement may go up two, three, four, or even more levels for resolution. The more the two functions depends on one another, the less efficient the process is. While the organization is trying to resolve the dispute, the customer sits, cools her heels, and begins to wonder why she shouldn't take her business elsewhere.

In an empowered, creative organization, by contrast, the two units, no matter where they're located, are empowered—and expected—to coordinate successfully at their level. It's the leader's job not to settle their disagreements but to see that they have the information and authority they need to settle them. And then to ensure that they do, in fact, settle them. At least initially, this may be far harder than playing Solomon and making the decision. But as empowerment becomes institutionalized, the leader's time is freed for far more productive work.

Communicating requires the same support. In a traditional organization, communication travels one way: down. Not so in a highly adaptive, creative organization. Sure, communication downward occurs in this organization, but so does communication upward and, most important of all, sideward. While there's more to communicating than just coordinating, coordinating can't happen without full communication.

Once again, a leader doesn't have to do the communicating. But he must create an environment that not only encourages but permits communication. Increasingly, this requires him to be more and more familiar with current technology—because E-mail systems, internal bulletin boards, teleconferencing systems, and a host of other technologies can facilitate the communicating process beyond the capabilities of even the *Enterprise* of the 1960s *Star Trek* series. Other people do the communicating, but the leader has to make it happen.

How does she do this? First of all, she sets the example by communicating openly and effectively herself. She lays her cards on the table and expects everyone else to do the same. She particularly makes it clear that she expects everyone to tell it like it is—and to ask the questions necessary to find out how it is. She expects the organization's members to react as sensible people, and so she shares good news as well as bad. She equally expects to *hear* the bad news as well as the good. She ensures that messengers never get shot and that those who identify the problems are never branded as troublemakers.

She also leads the way in including the organization's customers and suppliers in the communication loops and even in the decision-making processes themselves. She helps the organization be honest with its customers and suppliers, and in turn expects honesty from them. She understands the potential for problems when organizations build relationships this close with customers and suppliers, so she ensures that mutual trust is built and maintained (just as she does within the organization) and that appropriate safeguards exist. But her overriding concern is that communication occur on the freest and widest scale possible.

Finally, she's always available to talk with people. A manager once said of Stanley Gault, the immensely successful CEO first of Rubbermaid and then of Goodyear, that he never really told anyone what to do but they always knew what he wanted. I suspect that Mr. Gault is very adept at simply talking with people, listening to them, letting them bounce ideas off him, critiquing and commenting but never criticizing or condemning. I know that this often seems to be my role, and that I end discussion after discussion by saying "This is your call; do what you think best now and I'll support you." It works, and it seems to be a crucial part not only of communicating but of aligning the organization with the mission and coordinating its various activities.

Learning and Creating as an Organization

Whatever else the leader does, his ultimate goal is to focus the organization's energies on these two areas. I say "ultimate goal," because mission, trust, coordinating, and communicating always come first. In the short run, they make or break the organization. In the long run, though, the organization prospers only when it learns continually—and to accomplish this it must create continually.

We've dealt with both these topics before; there's no need to repeat what's already been said. Let me emphasize, however, that the more you can turn your organization's members into entrepreneurs, the more both learning and creativity will increase.

Peter Senge and others have stressed that teams are the most effective learning units. I agree with this to a point, but then I add a different stress. Teams will be creative and learn the more entrepreneurial they are, but it doesn't require a team as we usually understand it to do either. Let me explain.

In Chapter 3, I emphasized that creative organizations promote ownership and entrepreneurship everywhere, and ownership supports learning and creativity as nothing else can. Typical organizations are infected with the NIH—"not invented here"—syndrome. Pilot projects sound like a great idea, but other organizations always have a dozen reasons not to repeat what was piloted. Because failures are so risky, safe decisions are the order of the day; certainly there's no creativity or learning here.

Now look at an individual, team, group, or small organization with ownership of its results and rewards for achieving them. It may be bringing a new service to market, redesigning a critical process, even gearing up a brand-new start-up sponsored by the organization. Can it afford to reject effective ideas just because they came from somewhere else? Can it afford to take the safe route? Of course not. It must learn as quickly as it can, and be as creative as it can, to succeed.

The leader's job is to create organizational situations in which creativity and learning are rewarding and then to see that individuals are empowered to achieve the rewards. The more that ownership and entrepreneurship are encouraged and rewarded, the more deeply creativity and learning will be institutionalized as a way of life, as the ordinary way that things are done, as "nothing special."

After all these serious words, however, I have to remind you that creative organizations encourage play, daydreaming, and even silliness. Just as routine operations dull both creativity and learning, so an entrepreneurial environment can build monumental levels of stress. Sooner or later, stress takes its toll, and creativity starts to bleed away. Don't let it! One of your fundamental responsibilities as tireless proponent of creativity and learning is to counter stress with enthusiasm, celebration, play, daydreaming, silliness—whatever it takes to maintain the creative, learning edge.

The Core: Creative Intent

Any empowered organization must be led by individuals who develop and align the organization with the mission, develop and maintain trust, ensure that coordinating and communicating occur, and encourage creativity and learning. What truly makes an organization creative and keeps it that way, though, is *creative intent*. Only the leader can infuse the organization with this intent and keep it burning brightly no matter what the circumstances.

The last few decades have witnessed the broad impact of psychology on organizational thought. Unfortunately, as helpful as this may be, it has brought with it seemingly endless methods of manipulation. Some are overt; many works on behavior modification and on human relations tend in this direction. Others are more covertly manipulative; vision often seems to be a way of enticing, even seducing, employees into happy compliance with the organization's goals.

Ultimately, human life is successful only when it is lived intentionally. Ultimately, organizational members will do what they intend to do—*and no one intends to be manipulated*. A creative leader's final task is not manipulating the organization into creativity but the far more demanding and productive one of seeding creative intent throughout the organization. Without this intent, all the goals, systems, processes and what-have-you discussed in this book will ultimately fail. But when this intent is present, it will find ways to express itself. Where no structures exist to support it, members who intend to be creative will develop the structures. Where goals are too easy, members who intend to be creative will develop harder, more challenging goals.

In short, when an organization is infused with the irresistible force of creative intent, supposedly immovable objects don't have a chance.

What to Do Now

I'd like to end by making five very specific suggestions:

1. You now have a clear idea of what's involved in bringing a constantly creative organization to life and keeping it alive. You also have a clear idea of your organization's readiness to become constantly creative. Now's the time to make the hard decision: Is this something to which you're prepared to devote an immense amount of effort? Developing a constantly creative organization is not just one management responsibility among many. If you are to do it successfully, you must make it your *principal* responsibility. Everything else you do will become simply the way you are exercising this responsibility at a particular moment. With all the problems your organization faces, all the important matters fighting for your attention, are you really prepared to make so deep a commitment? Then, as they say in survey forms, if you answer yes, go on to item 2.

2. Next, survey your organization with a cold and objective gaze. Where are the strengths you can build on? Where are the obstacles, and where are the black holes into which your best efforts may vanish? Don't look only at units or teams, look at individuals too. Where will your allies come from, the players who will fight the necessary skirmishes day after day? Who will see constant creativity as just another "flavor of the month" and try to hunker down and ignore it until it passes? Get a basic sense of where you can initiate a creative system and whom you can depend on to support it. Be very selective. Don't attempt to change the whole organization at once.

3. Now that you've done the mental exercise, check out your conclusions. You especially need to know if the people you thought you could depend on will be there for you. You also need to test the water among some of those you expect to oppose what you're beginning; there might be a pleasant surprise or two here.

Don't rush this stage. Even individuals who may become enthusiastic supporters of your initiative may initially react with caution and ask some of the hardest questions. Bring up the idea in informal discussions, listen carefully to the objections, and be honest in your answers. Too much is at stake for anyone to wear rosy-colored glasses. This is the beginning of the development stage, which requires both enthusiastic support *and* hard-nosed criticism.

4. Once you have the support you need and have decided on the areas for the first implementation, you face one last problem: Is there time to do the operating work that must be done *and* to start moving toward continual creativity? While I hope becoming more creative will give you a high payoff from the beginning, I can't promise it will. Typically, even new programs that are implemented with the best intentions reach a stage at which the time required to produce the change runs headlong into the time needed for the basic work of the organization. How will you handle this? Can it be handled? Again, both enthusiasm and hard-nosed criticism are the order of the day.

5. Here's another way to look at your basic task: You must convince everyone who is key to the organization's success that this is not another "flavor of the month." Most organizations have tried several "bold new initiatives" over the past decade, and a very high percentage of these have failed to produce results. This happens particularly in areas whose managers or executives move every two or three years. Someone gets a program going and then leaves; her successor comes in, pays lip service to the program, and starts one of his own. (Remember, few managers ever got promoted for finishing something their predecessors began.) Your words, no matter how eloquent, will be drowned out by your actions. If you've really made the decision to become a constantly creative organization, start living it.

Let me conclude on a positive and, I hope, helpful note. The success or failure of change depends on those who must change. It is *not* true that people automatically resist change; that's a cop-out. However, whether they support or oppose it, people do find change *uncomfortable*. Here are seven steps you can take to make the changes you propose as comfortable as possible for your organization.

1. When performers, including managers, see the proposed change as a burden, they will resist it. Minimize the resistance by implementing the change in a way that will be a challenge for them.
2. When the payoff for the individual and the organization is unclear, trivial, or vague, the change will be resisted. Minimize the resistance by implementing the change in such a way that the payoff from it is seen as clear, worthwhile, and real.
3. To the extent that the change takes time to show results, it will be resisted. Minimize the resistance by implementing the change in stages so that it begins producing positive results quickly.
4. To the extent that the change involves multiple functions or departments, it will be resisted. Minimize the resistance by limiting the initial change to the fewest number of functions or departments possible. (One is best.)
5. To the extent that the change conflicts with existing status and power relationships, it will be resisted. Minimize the resistance by fitting the change to these relationships as fully as possible without compromising the goals of the change.
6. To the extent that the change conflicts with existing individual and organizational values, it will be resisted. Minimize the resistance by designing and presenting the change so that it affirms these values to the maximum extent possible—again, without compromising the goals of the change.
7. To the extent that the change seems uncertain and perhaps just another "flavor of the month," it will be resisted. Minimize the resistance by walking your talk from the beginning and *never* delegating basic responsibility for the change to anyone else.

I hope I've helped. Now it's up to you. Good luck.

Afterword:
Is Creativity Really
That Important?

Building a new kind of organization, one that maintains its frame flexibility, encourages diversity, and deals openly with conflict—is it really worth all this just for an organization to be creative? I can answer that question for me (yes!), but not for you. I do have a basic conviction on the issue. It led me to write this book, and I think now is the time for me to share it with you.

Several years ago, two social scientists, Henry Murray and Clyde Kluckhohn, coined the wonderful phrase that "any individual is like all others in some respects, like some others in some respects, and like no others in some respects."[1] In this book, I have dealt with diversity and conflict, based on the ways that we are like others in some respects and like no others in some respects. Underlying all this, however, is a basic conviction that all of us share a deep common humanness—and the core of this humanness is the desire and the ability to create.

I enjoy reading books on science, and I've read many written by authors deeply committed to showing that this or that aspect of the universe is "nothing but" some mechanical process. Perhaps so—but I know these three facts:

1. Once there was nothing; now there is an infinite universe of infinite complexity (and perhaps an infinite number of these universes).
2. Once there were only things; now there is life, existing from the bleakest mountain peak to the darkest part of the ocean floor.

3. Once life was blind, capable only of responding in simple, primitive ways to its immediate environment; now life is intelligent, capable of taking over evolution on its own, capable even of putting down humanity's most creative accomplishments as "nothing but. . . ."

I draw a simple conclusion from this: The most important point you can make about the universe is that it is creative. If this is so, then perhaps the most important point you can make about each of us is that we have this same creative power within us and we share the universe's desire to use it. Certainly almost all children, in virtually every known culture, are creative. And as our own culture focuses more and more on leisure, more and more of us attempt to fill this leisure time with creative activities.

I believe an organization should seek constant creativity because that is the greatest single contribution the people who compose it can make to its success. Not all of us to the same degree, and not any of us all the time, and certainly not in the same way. But creating something that works and solves a problem is a deep and probably unmatchable source of self-esteem, excitement, and commitment.

To paraphrase a line from the last chapter: Against the irresistible force of the universe's creative intent, there are no immovable objects.

Notes

Chapter 1:
What Makes an
Organization Creative?

1. M. Lewis Temares, in "Reality, Not Rhetoric," *Information Week*, June 7, 1993, p. 63.
2. Reflected, for instance, in *Fortune* magazine's lead article in the May 17, 1993, issue: "How We Will Work in the Year 2000" (pp. 38–52), and in books such as Robert Reich's *The Work of Nations* and Peter Drucker's *The Post-Capitalist Society*.
3. *The Fifth Discipline*, p. 14.
4. *Prophets in the Dark*, p. 87.
5. Just after I wrote these words, I discovered an interesting fact. Emerson has been moving slowly into higher-margin products; in the process, 23 percent of sales in 1992 were generated by products developed within the past five years (two and a half times the percentage in 1982). This level of creativity almost meets the 25 percent rate expected at 3M and Rubbermaid; apparently not even expert cost cutters are immune to the rapid changes in the marketplace. See Lois Therrien (with Richard A. Melcher), "A Knight with Thick Armor for IBM," *Business Week*, August 23, 1993, p. 28.
6. From a presentation by Ray Kordupleski at the June 1992 Conference of Organizational Systems Designers, Washington, D.C.
7. Hamper, *Rivethead*, pp. 61–64. I have had to edit the account significantly to keep it short; if it interests you, I strongly suggest that you read the original account. In fact, I recommend the entire book for a no-holds-barred look at a world most of us never experience.
8. While many individuals have stressed the importance of searching for opportunities rather than simply solving problems, I am indebted to Charlie Kiefer and Sherry Immediato of Innovation Associates for raising the issue in a new and more compelling way in their presentation at the June 1993 Conference of Organizational Systems Designers.
9. Several of the key ideas here are drawn from D. N. Perkins, *The Mind's Best Work*, and Getzels and Csikszentmihalyi, *The Creative Vision*. The first is much broader in scope than the second, but both make significant contributions to our understanding of the practice of creativity. Peter Drucker's *Innovation and Entrepreneurship* is also helpful for a fuller understanding of

some of these points. While I did not use them in preparing this chapter, pp. 300–303 of James Brian Quinn's *Intelligent Enterprise* deal with several common characteristics of innovation that research has uncovered.

10. Lt. Gen. William "Gus" Pagonis, in his account of the logistics support for the Gulf War, stresses again and again his conviction that combining clear goals with individual freedom to act was responsible for the incredible job that the United States did in moving and positioning materiel for the war. See William G. Pagonis, *Moving Mountains*.
11. From an address by Horst Schultze, April 8, 1993, Washington, D.C.
12. Katzenbach and Smith, *The Wisdom of Teams*, passim.
13. When Getzels and Csikszentmihalyi studied artists (in *The Creative Vision*), they found that the best single predictor of the success of a painting was the time the artist had taken defining the problem before he or she started to work. The greater the time spent in problem definition, the better the painting.
14. Farrell, *Searching for the Spirit of Enterprise*, pp. 163–64.

Chapter 2:
How Is an Organization a Creative System?

1. Asimov, *Forward the Foundation*, p. 23.
2. Peter Drucker has dealt with the value of unanticipated consequences at some length. See Chapter 3 of his *Innovation and Entrepreneurship*.
3. Dirk Cjelli explores the destructive aspects of combining control and resourcing in the same organization in "PT Confronts the Primal Bureaucratic Dysfunction," *Performance & Instruction*, August 1992, pp. 5–7. While semi-humorous, the article has a serious point.
4. Pagonis, *Moving Mountains*, p. 83. Gen. Pagonis goes on to add: "Concurrently, a wide variety of communication channels must be opened and cultivated, to ensure that these decentralized efforts add up to a coordinated whole." Chapter 3 of this book emphasizes just how important full communication is.
5. The first widely distributed book on quality, Philip Crosby's *Quality Is Free*, defined quality as conformance to requirements—measured totally by tactical feedback. However, the original book on Total Quality Management, Kaoru Ishikawa's *What Is Total Quality Control?*, begins with identifying the customer's requirements—the goal of strategic feedback. This makes a significant difference in competitiveness. A company that identifies quality as first of all finding out what the customer wants can move easily from focusing on high-quality current products to designing desirable new products. This, in fact, is exactly what the major Japanese companies have done. (Compare, for instance, the success of the 1993 redesign of the Toyota Camry with the far more limited success of General Motors' redesigns in recent years.)
6. Kearns and Nadler describe Xerox's change to a TQM culture in detail in *Prophets in the Dark*. Kearns provides an important caveat to some of the

current indiscriminate emphasis on listening to customers: "[I]f all you do is respond to the current users of your product . . . they will tell you . . . [t]hey want the same thing that they already have but they want it to be more reliable and to cost less. It's only through an interaction of your ideas with your most forward-thinking customers that fresh concepts emerge" (p. 87).

Chapter 3:
Why You Must Cultivate
Frame Flexibility

1. If you'd like to see just how influential frames can be, read Gareth Morgan's *Images of Organization*. He identifies nine distinct frames or metaphors for looking at organizations and then illustrates the very different view of what's happening and what needs to be done that each frame produces.
2. See, for instance, Alan Wilkins's *Developing Corporate Character*.
3. As I write this, in the summer of 1993, Apple continues to be the Number 2 provider of personal computers in the world, but its profits are sagging even though its sales are increasing. The basic reason? Apple's monopoly on a user-friendly computer interface is eroding as Windows for IBM-compatible PCs becomes equally user-friendly. Consequently, Apple is forced to compete in a market where PCs are commodities—a brand-new experience for the company. In the words of Jim Impoco, "Apple is stuck between the present and the future, between today's cutthroat computer business and tomorrow's promising digital world" ("Shaken to the Core," *U.S. News & World Report*, July 5, 1993, pp. 38–40). Can Apple survive? Translation: Can Apple stretch or break its conventional frames to become the kind of company the new market needs? You'll know the answer better when you read this note than I did when I wrote it.
4. Quinn, *Intelligent Enterprise*, p. 78.
5. "Street Talk" section of *USA Today*, May 13, 1993, p. 3B .
6. Louis S. Richman, "How Jobs Die—and Are Born," *Fortune*, July 26, 1993, p. 26.

Chapter 4:
How to Use Diversity and
Conflict Creatively

1. Schwarz and Volgy, *Forgotten Americans*, p. 7.
2. Peters and Waterman identified an organization that used this combination of clear goals with the freedom to achieve them by various means as being simultaneously loose and tight. They identified this loose-tight structure as one of the eight basic principles of excellence. See *In Search of Excellence*, Chapter 12.

3. Quoted anonymously in Donald Schön, *The Reflective Practitioner*, p. 254. I have added the emphasis on the last sentence.

Chapter 5:
Do Creativity and Technology Require a Shotgun Marriage?

1. From Donald A. Norman, *Things That Make Us Smart*, p. 113. He coined the term *Grudin's Law* after Jonathan Grudin, who first proposed it. This book and Norman's earlier book *The Psychology of Everyday Things* are brilliant and highly readable analyses of how technologies are unnecessarily user-hostile.
2. Barbara Garson, in *The Electronic Sweatshop* (published in 1988), saw this as a trend: "Right now a combination of twentieth-century technology and nineteenth-century scientific management is turning the Office of the Future into the factory of the past. At first this affected clerks and switchboard operators, then secretaries, bank tellers and service workers. The primary targets are now professionals and managers " (p. 10). These comments are particularly relevant to the second principle for job design in creative organizations.
3. The system is the Aetna Management Process; for more information on it, see Gloria Geary, *Electronic Performance Support Systems*, pp. 249–51.
4. Norman, *Things That Make Us Smart*, pp. 11, 138.
5. Howard Gleckman, "The Technology Payoff," p. 59.
6. Michael Hammer and James Champy, *Reengineering the Corporation*, is the current bible on reengineering. However, pages 158–64 of James Brian Quinn's *Intelligent Enterprise* present a brief but effective summary of the advantages of reengineering.
7. See, for instance, The National Center on Education and the Economy's report, *America's Choice: high skills or low wages!*
8. Garson, *The Electronic Sweatshop*, p. 13.
9. Zuboff, *In the Age of the Smart Machine*, pp. 5–6. Zuboff, who is not as pessimistic as Garson, goes on to paint an alternative approach: "Imagine the alternative: The new technological milieu becomes a resource from which are fashioned innovative methods of information sharing and social exchange. These methods in turn produce a deepened sense of collective responsibility and joint ownership, as access to ever-broader domains of information lend new objectivity to data and preempt the dictates of hierarchical authority" (p. 6). As you can see, the ideas I'm presenting are very similar at points to Zuboff's ideas of what must be done to create this alternative scenario. This is hardly an accident, since I (and many, many others) consider her book and its analysis to be a major contribution to the application of technology to work.
10. For a detailed account, see Geary, pp. 67–75.
11. See Quinn, *Intelligent Enterprise*, p. 111.
12. I devoted all of Chapter 7 of my book *Smart Training* to an in-depth analysis of why an organization needs its value-adding jobs to be highly skilled and vice versa. If you're still not clear about how important this is, you might want to read that chapter.

James Brian Quinn is a strong advocate of outsourcing not only inessential, routine jobs but all jobs that the company cannot perform at a world-class level. He advocates the position strongly throughout *Intelligent Enterprise*, but especially on pp. 380–95.

13. Norman, *Things That Make Us Smart*, p. 35. My own list is influenced by the list that Norman gives on pp. 34–35. However, the basis for much of his list and of mine is the work of Mihaly Csikszentmihalyi, professor of psychology at the University of Chicago. His two books most relevant to human performance are *Beyond Boredom and Anxiety* and *Flow*. The latter is more popularly written and contains research results not in the former. The basic results of his approach as they apply to work design have been outlined in Jay Huntingdon Hume, "Can We 'Go with the Flow' at Work?" *Performance & Instruction*, February 1992, pp. 49–52. In addition, Shoshana Zuboff's concept of "informating" as opposed to "automating" is also very relevant here. See *In the Age of the Smart Machine*.

14. Norman, p. 35.

15. The information about the credit card issuer is from a personal communication. The information on the stock market comes from a number of fragmentary sources.

Chapter 6:
How Can You Have Creativity, Reliability, and Efficiency?

1. If you're familiar with the S-curve used by Richard Foster in *Innovation: The Attacker's Advantage* (New York: Summit, 1986) to describe innovation, you'll find my interpretation of the innovation cycle similar in many (though not all) respects. Both the S-curve and the innovation cycle attempt to picture the law of diminishing returns as it applies to innovation.

2. Susan Moffat, "Japan's New Personalized Production," *Fortune*, October 22, 1990, p. 132.

3. Quoted in Tom Peters, *Thriving on Chaos*, pp. 167–68. Peters is quoting from Alan M. Kantrow, "Wide-open Management at Chaparral Steel," *Harvard Business Review*, May/June 1986, pp. 99–101. The emphasis on the last statement was added by Peters.

4. Which led him to call his first solo book *Thriving on Chaos*.

Chapter 7:
How to Get and Keep Creative Players

1. I deal with this and related training themes in *Smart Training*. The thesis of the book is that training should be designed to improve specific performance, not to transmit "nice-to-know" or "maybe useful someday" information to individuals.

2. Carl Sewell understands this clearly. This is how his auto dealerships do it:

> After we hire people they attend a new employee orientation meeting—where we talk about our history and how we expect our people to treat customers—and we assign everyone a "training partner," someone who's doing the same job they are and from whom they can learn company policy, or maybe just where the restroom is. When you're in a strange new situation, there's nothing better than having a friend, someone who can explain to you the folklore, culture, and rituals.
>
> We also try to communicate to our new employees who our heroes are, people who exemplify success around here. [Carl Sewell, *Customers for Life*, p. 74.]

3. Quoted in Quinn, *Intelligent Enterprise*, p. 152.

Chapter 8:
How Teams Promote Creativity

1. For a recent example, see Katzenbach and Smith, *The Wisdom of Teams*.
2. See, for instance, the accounts of Litel Communications and American Transtech in my earlier book, *Teampower*.
3. Let me insert a warning here. *Multiskilled* teams differ sharply from *multifunctional* teams. Members of multiskilled teams can perform most or all of the individual tasks on the team; members of multifunctional teams still perform primarily their own functions but work together with individuals from other functions. Multiskilled teams succeed when they perform relatively low-skilled work, since the combined tasks often make work far more interesting. When work is highly skilled to begin with, though, attempting to make the performers multiskilled generally produces serious cognitive overload. See my *Teampower* for a more detailed discussion.
4. The characteristics, only eight in number at that time, are presented at length in Chapter 2 of the book.

Chapter 9:
Why a Learning Organization
Must Be a Creative Organization

1. Richard Schonberger was one of the first to understand why Japanese feedback systems so often work better than Western ones. His book *Japanese Manufacturing Techniques* describes the differences in some detail—and, while he does not explicitly use the six characteristics, his description makes their relevance clear.

Chapter 10:
How Do You Manage a Constantly Creative Organization?

1. I have been kinder to the PODC model than I believe it deserves. I thought the model was basically flawed when I first ran into it in the 1960s, and nothing has happened in my twenty-some years as a manager since then to change this opinion.

Afterword:
Is Creativity Really That Important?

1. Quoted in Wallace and Gruber, *Creative People at Work*, p. 26. The reference to Murray and Kluckhohn is to their work *Personality in Nature, Society, and Culture* (New York: Alfred A. Knopf, 1950).

Bibliography

Albrecht, Karl, with Steven Albrecht. *The Creative Corporation.* Homewood, IL: Dow Jones-Irwin, 1987.

Asimov, Isaac. *Forward the Foundation* (the final book in the Foundation series). New York: Doubleday, 1993.

Carr, Clay. "Managing Self-Managing Teams," *Training and Development*, September 1991, pp. 36–42.

———. *The New Manager's Survival Manual: All the Skills You Need for Success.* New York: John Wiley & Sons, 1989.

———. "Performance Technology in the Bionic Organization," *Performance & Instruction*, October 1989 through August 1990.

———. *Smart Training: The Manager's Guide to Training for Improved Performance.* New York: McGraw-Hill, 1992.

———. *Teampower: Lessons from America's Top Companies on Putting Teampower to Work.* Englewood Cliffs, NJ: Prentice Hall, 1992.

Charlotte, Susan, with Tom Ferguson and Bruce Felton. *Creativity: Conversations with 28 Who Excel.* Troy, MI: Momentum Books, 1993.

Cjelli, Dirk. "PT Confronts the Primal Bureaucratic Dysfunction." *Performance & Instruction*, August 1992, pp. 5–7.

Crosby, Philip B. *Quality Is Free.* New York: The New American Library, 1980.

Csikszentmihalyi, Mihaly. *Beyond Boredom and Anxiety: The Experience of Play in Work and Games.* San Francisco: Jossey-Bass, 1977.

———. *Flow: The Psychology of Optimal Experience.* New York: Harper & Row, 1990.

Davidow, William H., and Michael S. Malone. *The Virtual Corporation: Lessons from the World's Most Advanced Companies.* New York: HarperCollins, 1992.

Drucker, Peter F. *Innovation and Entrepreneurship.* New York: Harper, 1985.

———. *The Post-Capitalist Society.* New York: Harper, 1993.

Fisher, Roger, and William Ury. *Getting to Yes: Negotiating Agreement without Giving In.* Boston: Houghton Mifflin, 1981.

Garson, Barbara. *The Electronic Sweatshop: How Computers Are Transforming the Office of the Future into the Factory of the Past.* New York: Simon and Schuster, 1988.

Geary, Gloria J. *Electronic Performance Support Systems: How and Why to Remake the Workplace through the Strategic Application of Technology.* Boston: Weingarten, 1991.

Getzels, Jacob W., and Mihaly Csikszentmihalyi. *The Creative Vision: A Longitudinal Study of Problem Finding in Art.* New York: Wiley-Interscience, 1976.

Gleckman, Howard. "The Technology Payoff," *Business Week,* June 14, 1993, pp. 57–68.

Hammer, Michael, and James Champy. *Reengineering the Corporation: A Manifesto for Business Revolution.* New York: Harper Business, 1993.

Hamper, Ben. *Rivethead: Tales from the Assembly Line.* New York: Warner, 1990.

Hume, Jay Huntingdon. "Can We 'Go with the Flow' at Work?" *Performance & Instruction,* February 1992, pp. 49–52.

Imai, Masaaki. *Kaizen: The Key to Japan's Competitive Success.* New York: Random House Business Division, 1986.

Ishikawa, Kaoru, *What Is Total Quality Control?: The Japanese Way.* Translated by David J. Lu. Englewood Cliffs, NJ: Prentice-Hall, 1985.

Katzenbach, Jon R., and Douglas K. Smith. *The Wisdom of Teams: Creating the High-Performance Organization.* Boston: Harvard Business School Press, 1993.

Kearns, David T., and David A. Nadler. *Prophets in the Dark: How Xerox Reinvented Itself and Beat Back the Japanese.* New York: Harper Business, 1992.

Lipnack, Jessica, and Jeffrey Stamps. *The Teamnet Factor: Bringing the Power of Boundary Crossing Into the Heart of Your Business.* Essex Junction, VT: Oliver Wight Publications, 1993.

Marshall, Ray, and Marc Tucker. *Thinking for a Living: Education and the Wealth of Nations.* New York: Basic Books, 1992.

Michalko, Michael. *Thinkertoys: A Handbook of Business Creativity for the 90s.* Berkeley, CA: 10-Speed Press, 1991.

Mindell, Arnold. *The Leader as Martial Artist.* New York: Bantam, 1992.

Mitroff, Ian I., and Harold A. Linstone. *The Unbounded Mind: Breaking the Chains of Traditional Business Thinking.* New York: Oxford, 1992.

Moffat, Susan. "Japan's New Personalized Production," *Fortune,* October 22, 1990, p. 132.

Morgan, Gareth. *Images of Organization.* Newbury Park, CA: Sage, 1986.

National Center on Education and The Economy. *America's Choice: high skills or low wages!* Rochester, NY: 1990.

Norman, Donald A. *The Psychology of Everyday Things.* New York: Basic Books, 1986.

————. *Things That Make Us Smart: Defending Human Attributes in the Age of the Machine.* Reading, MA: Addison-Wesley, 1993.

Ohmae, Kenichi. *The Mind of the Strategist: Business Planning for Competitive Advantage.* New York: Viking Penguin, 1983.

Oncken, William. *Managing Management Time.* Englewood Cliffs, NJ: Prentice-Hall, 1986.

Pagonis, William G. *Moving Mountains: Lessons in Leadership and Logistics from the Gulf War.* Boston: Harvard Business School Press, 1992.

Perkins, D. N. *The Mind's Best Work.* Cambridge, MA: Harvard University Press, 1981.

Peters, Thomas J. *Thriving on Chaos.* New York: Alfred A. Knopf, 1987.

Peters, Thomas J., and Robert H. Waterman, Jr. *In Search of Excellence: Lessons from America's Best-Run Companies.* New York: Harper, 1982. Paperback edition published by Warner Books, 1983.

Quinn, James Brian. *Intelligent Enterprise: A New Paradigm for a New Era.* New York: Free Press, 1992.

Reich, Robert B. *The Work of Nations: Preparing Ourselves for 21st Century Capitalism.* New York: Alfred A. Knopf, 1991.

Russo, J. Edward, and Paul J. H. Schoemaker. *Decision Traps: The Ten Barriers to Brilliant Decision-Making and How to Overcome Them.* New York: Fireside (Simon & Schuster), 1990.

Schaffer, Robert H. *The Breakthrough Strategy: Using Short-Term Successes to Build the High Performance Organization.* Cambridge, MA: Ballinger, 1988.

Schön, Donald A. *The Reflective Practitioner: How Professionals Think in Action.* New York: Basic Books, 1983.

Schonberger, Richard J. *Japanese Manufacturing Techniques: Nine Hidden Lessons in Simplicity.* New York: Free Press, 1982.

Schwarz, John E., and Thomas J. Volgy. *Forgotten Americans: Thirty Million Working Poor in the Land of Opportunity.* New York: W. W. Norton, 1992.

Semler, Ricardo. *Maverick: The Success Story Behind the World's Most Unusual Workplace.* New York: Warner, 1993.

Senge, Peter M. *The Fifth Discipline: The Art & Practice of the Learning Organization.* New York: Doubleday, 1990.

Sewell, Carl, with Paul B. Brown. *Customers for Life: How to Turn That One-Time Buyer into a Lifetime Customer.* New York: Doubleday (Currency), 1990.

Short, Ron. *A Special Kind of Leadership: The Key to Learning Organizations.* Seattle: The Leadership Group, 1991.

Theobald, Robert. *Turning the Century: Personal and Organizational Strategies for Your Changed World*. Indianapolis: Knowledge Systems, 1992.

Thomas, R. Roosevelt. *Beyond Race and Gender: Unleashing the Power of Your Total Work Force by Managing Diversity*. New York: AMACOM, 1991.

Ury, William. *Getting Past No: Negotiating with Difficult People*. New York: Bantam, 1991.

VanGundy, Arthur B. *Idea Power: Techniques & Resources to Unleash the Creativity in Your Organization*. New York: AMACOM, 1992.

Wallace, Doris B., and Howard E. Gruber. *Creative People at Work*. New York: Oxford, 1989.

Weeks, Dudley. *The Eight Essential Steps to Conflict Resolution: Preserving Relationships at Work, at Home, and in the Community*. Los Angeles: Jeremy Tarcher, 1992.

Wilkins, Alan L. *Developing Corporate Character: How to Successfully Change an Organization Without Destroying It*. San Francisco: Jossey-Bass, 1989.

Womack, James P., Daniel T. Jones, and Daniel Roos. *The Machine That Changed the World*. New York: Rawson Associates (Macmillan), 1990.

Zuboff, Shoshana. *In the Age of the Smart Machine: The Future of Work and Power*. New York: Basic Books, 1988.

Index